SCOTLAND YARD WITH PAL

F THE BANQUETING-HOUSE.

THE STORY OF SCOTLAND YARD

This authentic story of Scotland Yard takes the reader behind
the scenes of one of the most remarkable law enforcement
agencies in the world. Writing in collaboration with serving
Yard detectives and uniformed police officers, Laurence
Thompson gives a fascinating, first-hand account of the inner
workings of the Yard's various branches. He describes such
departments as the crime car and river patrols, the science
laboratories, the fingerprint department, and the well-known
C.I.D., showing how they cooperate to form the force that
has tackled some of the most baffling crimes in history.

Authoritative, exciting and dramatic, this is an intriguing
study of the hundreds of crimes that were solved by the incredible courage and ingenuity of England's famous Scotland
Yard.

The Story of
SCOTLAND YARD

by LAURENCE THOMPSON

Illustrated with photographs

Random House   New York

Contents

Introduction

by Former Detective Supt. Robert Fabian

HAVE YOU EVER WONDERED WHAT WENT ON AT New Scotland Yard?

If you haven't, you will surely have been thrilled by newspaper headlines—"*Scotland Yard Has Been Called In*"—and wondered how it was possible for them to solve so many baffling problems.

Having served for twenty-eight years and five days in the Metropolitan Police—trained at Peel House and the Detective School at Hendon; worked the beats of the old Vine Street Police Station; carried out the duties of a detective in Central Office, C.R.O., "B", "C", "D" and "M" Divisions—and having been Chief Inspector in charge of the Flying Squad in addition to having been called in on numerous occasions by the Chief Constables of Provincial Police Forces to assist in the investigation of a murder or other serious crime, I am able to tell you that here is a book which is a pleasure to read, because the descriptions of the various departments at Scotland Yard and their functions are correct.

It has been said that: "Whenever a criminal commits a crime, Providence finds a witness."

Far be it from me to disagree with a well-known quotation. I was only thinking of the times I had to search for and find those witnesses! The chapters on the Criminal Record Office, the Finger Print Bureau and the Laboratory tell you how these are so often found.

As you will see when you read this book, the detective has at his disposal the assistance of the most learned men and women of the land.

In the case of a murder or suspicious death, what actually happens is that he appeals to the pathologist. . . . "Tell me," he says, "what were the causes of death?" "How long has the victim been dead?" "Do you think that the crime was committed here, or has the body been moved?" "What type of instrument do you think was the cause of death?"

In the case of death by poisoning the analyst will be appealed to. "What poison was used?" "How long before death was it administered?"

To the fingerprint expert he turns to know whether the impressions left at the scene of a crime are those of the victim or the criminal. If the latter, "Is he known?" If "Yes," then further inquiry is made at the Criminal Record Office, where the officer is asked: "What is he like?" "What is his or her description?" "Is there anything outstanding about him?"

The officer having been supplied with these details will inquire, "Tell me where he may be found, who are his associates?"

If no fingerprints are found, "Can C.R.O. tell me, on the facts so far, who may have committed the crime?"

To the officer in charge of telephones and wireless

the officer looks for speedy and accurate circulation of the facts he wishes to release. Perhaps the messages have to be flashed to all sea- and airports to warn Special Branch Officers (who are also members of the C.I.D.) to keep watch for a suspect likely to leave the country.

To the Scientific and Medical Specialist: "Here is some article belonging to the victim or assailant, some hairs or fibers found adhering to the victim"; or perhaps, "some instrument with which the crime may have been committed." The officer asks: "Is it blood; if so, is it human or animal?" If the former, "Is it the blood of the victim? If not, perhaps the suspect's? Are the hairs and fibers animal or human?"

The instrument is then taken to the photographic section. "Can you get some good pictures showing . . . ?"

Yes, there is no doubt that a detective's life is full of interest. No man's work is more varied or full of the unexpected. He goes into the homes of the highest and the lowest. He meets dukes and dustmen, bishops and pickpockets. He must be a good mixer and able to hold his own in any company. He must accumulate knowledge about all sorts of obscure things: banking, bookkeeping and company law for cases of fraud; anatomy, pathology and toxicology for cases of murder and the like; but most important of all, he must gain a deep knowledge of human nature. I am sure no more fascinating life can be offered to any man.

Finally, I would add, while commenting on the qualifications of a detective officer, the element of luck. I mean, you might go down one street and see nothing. If you go down the next street, you might fall over the best job in your service. What you have to do, of course, is to decide which is the best street to go down!

Detectives in real life are so different from the detectives of fiction—Sherlock Holmes, Dick Barton, etc. They marry and have families, but they have to be "married to their job." The detective has no regular hours, and can never say: "Well, thank goodness, I've finished for the day," because he knows by the time he has reached his home a message may be already waiting for him—"Please attend the office at once, re the case of——." Something has developed, and back he goes to take up a previous inquiry about which some urgent information has been received.

The chapters in this book which deal with the training of officers so took my mind back to the time I joined the police, that I thought it might be interesting to you to know exactly the steps one passes through to become a senior detective.

In early 1921 I applied to the Candidates' Branch at Scotland Yard for the necessary form of application to join the Metropolitan Police.

I filled up the form and took it to the local police station. Here they measured me and weighed me.

I remember what struck me most at my first sight

of the inside of a police station was how different the men looked without their helmets on—they became individuals instead of impassive arms of the law. There was also that indefinable police station smell, which even after 28 years I never can place properly—a mixture of scrubbing soap, disinfectant and type-writer ribbons.

On instruction, I attended the Recruiting Branch and passed the medical and educational examinations. The medical was stiff, the educational simple. On May 17th, 1921, I was finally "called up." At Peel House we were soon shaken up and allotted a cubicle.

Eight weeks of training followed—Police Duty, First Aid, Foot Drill, Self-defence, etc. Then came examinations, and on July 11th, 1921, we went to Scotland Yard, where the Stores Sergeant fitted us out with two of everything. I was then posted to Vine Street Police Station as Police Constable 118, "C" Division.

In those days we were posted night duty and put in charge of an experienced P.C. to show us round, to point out the boundaries of the beats, to make sure we noted the fire alarm posts, addresses of doc-tors, chemists, public houses, shops, churches and places of interest.

I remember being quite overwhelmed and wonder-ing whether I would ever master the job.

As time went on, however, I attended classes of instruction daily and passed the three-, six- and twelve-months' examinations; then away to the life of a constable whose appointment has been confirmed.

In 1923 I applied to join the Criminal Investigation Department, and was brought out in plain clothes as "Aid to C.I.D." I thought, "Well, it is now or never," so I patrolled for my allotted hours and very many more as well. I came to know the West End of London like the back of my hand, and what is more I came to like the job. My first arrest for crime was made one evening when I was really off duty. I was strolling round with a girl friend and noticed two young men taking what I considered was too much interest in unattended motor cars. We followed them, and sure enough, in Sloane Street, well off my own Division, I saw them steal a rug from a car.

Well, with more study and examinations that I passed, gradually I crept up the ladder until, by July 1st, 1949, I was promoted to Detective Superintendent.

I have read most books about Scotland Yard, but have yet to read a more intimate and correct account than this one. It might well have been called "Behind the Scenes at Scotland Yard."

1

A Nose for Crime

"You get a nose for crime," said the observer of Metropolitan Police radio car 5D meditatively, as we cruised about the shadowy streets behind the Edgware Road. Even as he talked, his eyes never ceased glancing from one side of the road to the other, exploring doorways and dark alleys, looking for a window that might be open, or an approaching car with the number of one of those noted as stolen on the log-sheet before him. And beneath his voice was the voice of the radio from Scotland Yard: "Hallo, all cars, from M2GW. Message No. 32 from G.A. begins: Green Fordson fifteen—one fife—hundred-weight covered van QLA 193—Q for Queenie, L for Lucy, A for Andrew, 193—lost or stolen Latimer Road 2045 /2130 containing 30 cases of tinned fruit. Ends. Origin 2135."

Radio car 5D played her part in that justly famous police film, *The Blue Lamp*. In one year her crews made 368 arrests and headed the roll of honor of Metropolitan Police crime cars. She is a 17 h.p. Humber, black and sleek as rain-washed tarmac, and when her driver chooses to accelerate from cruising to chasing speed, you leave your stomach quite a long way behind you.

"Yes, you get a nose for crime," said the big police-man again, with his faint Devon burr which he has not lost even after 21 years in London. "Take a case like this. We got a radio call one night on the car here. Disturbance at an address near Paddington Station. That's all we're told. It may be a murder. It may just be somebody who's had a few drinks, kicking up a fuss outside a pub. It's our job to get there quickly, and sort it out.

"So we go along to this address. It's a big house, divided into flats. The landlady's on the ground floor, and she knows nothing about any disturbance. We go on upstairs. There's a girl there. She's been having a party with a couple of fellows, and now they've turned her out. Because of that, she's phoned for the police.

"Well, there's nothing we can do about that one. No one's committed any offence. We can just quiet her down, and go away. But I think I'd like to have a look inside. No particular reason. I'm inquisitive, that's all. I knock, and ask the tenant if he minds my coming in. Two chaps there. One of them's a little fellow, and when he sees me the blood drains out of his face. 'Hallo, chummy,' I think. 'What's the matter with you?' I ask some questions. Identity cards. Chummy's lost his. Has he reported it? Yes, he has, but he doesn't seem very sure what police station he reported it at. Has he served with the forces? No, he was exempt, he's an engineer. Where? He says he works for his dad, in a garage.

"Well, they don't exempt that kind of engineer, and anyway I look at his hands and see he's never done a dirty day's work in his life. So I think it over, and tell chummy I've reason to believe he's a deserter, and I'm going to take him to the police station. 'All right,' he says, 'but let me pack a few things to take along with me.' He packs his bag, and by this time I'm so certain there's something wrong I telephone Criminal Record Office at the Yard, to find if they've anything on a chap with the name chummy's given me. They haven't, but I take him along to the station just the same.

"He tells me his identity card was issued in York, with such-and-such a number. I telephone York. Right number, wrong name. I ask chummy a few more questions. After a couple of hours he tells me his name. I phone C.R.O. again—anything known against him? 'I should say so,' they tell me. 'He's been a deserter four years, and we want him for about thirty robberies. He's pinched eight thousand quids' worth of stuff.' And believe it or not, the bag he packed to bring along to the station was full of stuff he'd pinched only the night before!

"There you are. And yet some people won't be-lieve you when you say you get a nose for crime."

The observer of crime car 5D is an ordinary police-constable, and he and his like are the reason why London is the best-policed city in the world. He calls it "having a nose for crime," and because the police are not given to boasting, he makes it sound as easy as catching the 8:25 train to the office every morning. In later chapters of this book you are going inside Scotland Yard, headquarters of the Metropolitan Police. You will see the crime cars at work, the river patrols, the dogs and horses, the policemen on their beats and the detectives of the Criminal Investigation Department. You will visit the Information Room from which radio messages go to the police cars, and the Criminal Record Office. You will meet the white-coated scientists in their laboratory analyzing the dust from a safe-breaker's turned-up trousers, the fingerprint men hanging a murderer with their expert evidence.

You will see the whole machine for the prevention and detection of crime at work, ruthless, sure and endlessly persevering. You will find the real thing more fascinating than the best detective fiction ever written. And when you have finished, you will be able to say whether or not you think it is "easy."

But we must begin at the beginning, and the beginning is a long time ago.

2

Scotland Yard's First Detective

TODAY, WHEN THE POLICEMAN IS THE FIRST PERSON we go to when we are in trouble, when he is sometimes our next door neighbor, it is difficult for

us to imagine a large city without policemen. But in
the early part of the 18th century, London *was* without proper policemen. Behind the rich and fashion-
able houses in Covent Garden, Piccadilly and Blooms-
bury, within a stone's throw of the rich merchants'
homes in the City, beneath the shadow of Wren's
new Cathedral of St. Paul's, lay another city. This
was a city of poverty, of squalid courts a few feet
wide, leading from one to the other, between tight-
packed, overhanging hovels, a few of brick and stone,
but many of wood.

When there was a hue and cry after a criminal,
he dodged from court to narrow court, climbing over
the sloping roofs while his friends did their best to
trip or knife the handful of "thief-takers" who came
after him.

A few years later Henry Fielding, the famous
novelist who became a Bow Street magistrate, made
a night raid on two cottages in Shoreditch which
were known as the resort of criminals. He found
seventy men, women and children packed away in
their stinking, tiny rooms. All these people, including little children of five and six who were trained
as pickpockets, were "wanted" for crime.

Such conditions made criminals. Typical of them
was Jack Sheppard, whose execution in 1724, when
he was 22, was watched by 200,000 people. Sheppard,
the son of honest working people, was apprenticed
to a respectable trade. He ran away from it because
he fancied he had been ill-treated, and found it easy

to make more money by thieving than his father had done by a lifetime of honest work.

Highwaymen committed robbery in broad daylight, in the sight of a crowd, and rode solemnly and triumphantly through the town without danger or molestation. If they were chased, there were twenty or thirty armed men ready to come to their assistance. Murder was an everyday affair, and there were many people who made heroes of the murderers.

So young Jack Sheppard became a petty thief, then a highwayman. He was a boy still in his teens, 5 feet 4 inches tall, very slender and pale, tight-lipped, with no future to hope for except the gallows or a rival's bullet.

Working behind most of the thieves were the receivers of the stolen property, as there are today. One of the biggest was Jonathan Wild. Most of the thieves and rogues of London worked for him, and he organized them in gangs like an army, with their own officers. One gang's job was to rob on the main roads into London, one covered the churches, and one was for entertainments and public functions. A special brigade was set up to find employment as servants and then pilfer or open the doors at night for other robbers to enter. Jonathan Wild also had a staff of mechanics for altering watches and jewelry, warehouses to store the loot, and a sloop to convey stolen goods across to the continent where they could be more safely sold.

All the property which was stolen came to Wild.

Then he advertised it as "recovered," and sold it back to the owners; or, if they did not claim it, he sold it elsewhere. His activities became so widespread that a special act was passed, making the receiver of stolen goods an accessory to the theft. Wild got around this by opening a "Lost Property Office," at which those who had had goods stolen might report their loss. Wild charged them a fee for making inquiries about the theft—and of course another fee for reclaiming the goods which he had "found."

The authorities might have taken stronger steps against Wild if he had not been so useful as a "thief-taker." He knew every criminal, employed most of them, and when it suited his purpose, or because he wanted to get rid of a dangerous man, he would hand some rogue over to the authorities for hanging. In this way he made more money, for there was generally a reward on each criminal's head. Wild also kept discipline among his gangs, for every man knew that if he disobeyed the boss he would be betrayed and would quickly find himself on the gallows.

Jack Sheppard, who had robbed for Wild and killed honest men so that Wild might grow rich, fell out with the boss and was duly betrayed to the authorities.

While he was awaiting trial, which was certain to end in death, this slender, pale boy of 22 broke out of Newgate Prison. He accomplished this by getting rid of the irons with which his wrists and ankles were shackled, cutting through a double grille of oak and iron bars, descending 25 feet by a knotted sheet and blanket, and climbing a 22-foot wall with a companion on his back. He was caught, tried and condemned. He escaped again, however, and walked openly about the London underworld, where he was well known but where no man dared raise a hand to him for fear of his ever-ready pistols.

He was caught once more, taken to a stronger part of the prison known as The Castle, and there chained with two ponderous staples to the floor. A third time he freed himself of his manacles, snapped the chains that held him to the floor, removed a heavy iron bar from the chimney, and climbed up it. Forcing the heavily bolted doors of several rooms, he found himself on the upper leads of the prison, with a 20-foot drop to the next house. He had no means of crossing it, so he coolly went back to his cell, took a blanket, and with that swung across to safety.

But though he might escape from chains and prisons and bars, he could not escape from being Jack Sheppard. There was nowhere for him to go, so he spent his time in his usual drinking dens, and when drunk he was caught for the last time, and hanged.

To cope with criminals like Jack Sheppard and Jonathan Wild, there were no organized police as we know them today. There were the "Charleys," the watchmen so named because they had been established in Charles II's reign. These were generally old, feeble men, fit to go about the streets calling out "Past three o'clock and a cold, frosty morning," but not much use against Jack Sheppard's two pistols. One of these ancient creatures did arrest a man, and kept him under arrest for twelve hours, too—for smoking a cigar in the street. Another was appealed to by a man whose hat had been snatched under the watchman's very eyes. When asked to chase the thief the watchman refused. The reason? The other side of the road, where the thief was running, was not on his beat!

There were also constables. The modern English police are called police constables, and it is an old and honorable name derived from *comes stabuli*, the Master of the Horse of the Eastern Roman Emperors at Byzantium. From as early as 1252, one or more constables had been appointed for each parish in England. It was a position of honor, going to men who today would be local councillors, trade union officials, justices of the peace, and so on.

But the work was unpaid, and the constables were not expected to do more than carry out the law in sleepy country towns and villages, where the commonest crime was the theft of Mrs. Jones's washing from the hedge on which it was drying. In such a growing town as London, where the work became more and more difficult and dangerous, the men who should have done it paid others, less respectable and less efficient, to do it for them. It was part of the constable's duty to raise the "hue and cry" after an escaping criminal, causing all passers-by to join in the pursuit. But not many unarmed passers-by could be persuaded to help an unarmed constable tackle an armed and trigger-happy Jack Sheppard. Anyway, in the drinking dens where Jack Sheppard was likely to be, the passers-by were generally on Jack Sheppard's side.

Finally there were the justices of the peace. Many of them were "trading justices," needy men who had bought their justiceships as an investment, and had to make a living from them. They did this by such tricks as arresting innocent men, then delaying their trial until the prisoners ransomed themselves. These "trading justices" made their own arrests, with the help of bullies paid by themselves, who were sometimes recruited from Jonathan Wild's gangs; and Wild himself, if he was not actually a justice, certainly employed justices.

The English government did not organize a police force because the government was not then, as it is now, responsible through Parliament to democratic voters. It was answerable to no one but the Queen, and any police force which it organized would have been a political police force, as it was in France and other countries, concerned less with putting down crime than with arresting the government's political opponents.

The government would have been quite happy to put its political opponents into jail; but the question of who *was* the government depended only on the whims of Queen Anne. The government one day was Whig, because the Queen was friendly with the Duchess of Marlborough, who was a Whig; but the government next week might be Tory, because the Queen had fallen out with the Duchess of Marlborough and was friendly with the Tory Mrs. Masham. The government of one week therefore thought it safer not to have a police force which next week might be putting *them* in jail. And on the whole, since political police forces are easier to form than to get rid of, Jack Sheppard and Jonathan Wild were a cheap price to pay for freedom from such influences.

So it was left to four remarkable individuals to make their own arrangements for dealing with London's criminals. The first of these men was Thomas De Veil. Born in 1684, he was the son of French Protestant refugees. He, like Jack Sheppard, was apprenticed to a trade, and did not like it. He left his trade and joined Marlborough's armies as a private. He rose to the rank of captain, and returned to England from Spain as a half-pay officer. He was a vain, greedy, and ambitious man with expensive tastes and a desire to be on familiar terms with the "right people" in the London of his day.

His captain's half-pay did not help him far towards this, so he set up office to act as an agent between private citizens and government departments. In those days government departments generally had to be bribed before they would do what private citi-

zens wanted them to do. The place where De Veil
set up his office was a small yard at the top of Whitehall, which was then a part of the royal Palace of
Westminster. In older days it had been the site of
the house where Kings and Queens of Scotland lived
when they visited the English Court. It was known,
therefore, as Scotland Yard.

Captain De Veil—who soon became Colonel De
Veil because of his service in the Militia—did not
stay long in Scotland Yard. Through knowing the
right people, he was made a justice of the peace, and
moved his office to Bow Street. He was a "trading
justice"—that is, he made a living by selling justice
to those who could pay him for it. But because he
was ambitious, he also sought to make himself useful to the authorities, and because he wanted to be
accepted in the right circles, he did not follow the
path of Jonathan Wild.

He had the necessary courage to meet the Jack
Sheppards with their own weapons, and he broke
up several gangs like Wild's by armed raids, which
he led in person. There were many attempts to kill
him, and when he put into force an unpopular government order forbidding the sale of cheap gin, the
mob rioted and tried to lynch him, but he faced
them bravely, and was not harmed.

De Veil has been called the first detective, and
there are several stories of his prowess in examining
the criminals brought before him, and of his dogged
determination in pursuit of a murderer. A Mr. Drew,

for instance, a Suffolk lawyer, was shot dead in his own house, and though the murderer was suspected, there was no proof.

Meanwhile, in London, De Veil's attention had been drawn to the behavior of the dead man's son Charles, who was spending a great deal of money in London, getting into many scrapes, and showing no sign of mourning for his father. De Veil had Charles Drew before him and examined him closely. Not satisfied with Charles's story, he examined him again and again and again, until at last Charles broke down and confessed. De Veil thereupon packed him back to Suffolk to stand his trial, and was himself a leading witness for the prosecution.

On another occasion a suspected thief was brought before him. In answer to all De Veil's questions, the suspect refused to admit his guilt. De Veil therefore left him, and began casually to talk to other men in the room. Presently he asked the alleged thief if he had a knife with which to sharpen a pen. Unthinkingly, the man pulled out his knife. De Veil examined it, found the point broken off. "Go to the scene of the crime," he told two of his thief-takers, "and you will find a broken tip which will fit this blade." They did; and thus another criminal had made the mistake which sealed his doom.

De Veil left a tradition. He had held court in his own office at Bow Street like any of His Majesty's judges. The authorities decided that it might not be a bad thing to have a paid justice sitting permanently at Bow Street to deal with crime in the very heart of the great city. There is still a permanent magistrate at Bow Street, who is always Chief Magistrate of Westminster. But he is not a detective or a thief-taker, for it was soon decided that the magistrate, like His Majesty's judges, must be impartial, administering the law fairly for all, and not being policeman, prosecutor and judge all rolled into one.

De Veil was succeeded at Bow Street by Henry Fielding, the novelist, who had been trained as a barrister, and who continued De Veil's war against the gangs which sprang up one after another.

From Henry Fielding came the idea of regular armed patrols to meet the gangsters on their own ground with their own weapons. Henry Fielding did not himself set up these patrols. That was done by his half-brother and successor at Bow Street, Sir John Fielding. Sir John was born blind, yet despite his blindness, he was said to have known 3,000 criminals by the sounds of their voices.

Sir John organized the first Patroles, well-mounted men armed with cutlasses, pistols and truncheon, who policed the roads in parties within six miles of Charing Cross during the early and dangerous part of the night. At first these patrols were paid for by rich citizens, but later they were taken over by the government and their numbers increased. Their leather hats, blue coats with brass buttons, blue trousers and boots became as familiar on the roads as their warning cry of "Bow Street Patrole!" They are the ancestors of the Metropolitan Mounted Police, and of radio car 5D and its kind.

In 1797, the West India merchants whose rich cargoes came to the London docks along the Thames to be unloaded, lost £500,000-worth of goods through theft. The Heavy Horsemen, Light Horsemen, Long Apron Men, Scuffle Hunters, River Pirates, Mud Larks and Night Plunderers, as the river thieves were romantically named, won a rich plunder by snatching bales and crates from the docks, cutting barges adrift, and carrying away whole heavy anchors.

In the following year another London magistrate, Patrick Colquhoun, persuaded the merchants to pay for a boat patrol on the Thames to deal with this thieving. The Thames patrolmen were seamen or watermen, who manned long-oared gigs and were armed with blunderbuses and cutlasses. Within a year they had broken up the gangs.

Ten years afterward a private dock company at Wapping employed a River Police Officer to watch a ship which was being resheathed with copper. The company ordered ten bags of copper nails and 1,600 sheets of copper, the amount used for the same work before the river gangs' pilfering had been stopped. When the work was done, three bags of nails and 113 sheets of copper—the amount which would have been stolen before—were left over. This proved the effectiveness of the ancestors of the men who are today the Thames Division of the Metropolitan Police.

Now you begin to see Scotland Yard as we know it today, gradually taking shape. Like many English things it grew little by little to meet the changing needs of the times. But there is an important department of Scotland Yard whose beginnings we have not yet mentioned. That department is the C.I.D., and its ancestry goes back before the Mounted Patrols, before the River Police. The foundations of the Criminal Investigation Department may be seen in the Bow Street runners.

And Bow Street's Robin Redbreasts, with their scarlet waistcoats and brace of pistols, deserve a new chapter.

3

Runners and Peelers

WHEN HENRY FIELDING BEGAN HIS PLANS AT BOW Street for breaking up the gangs, his first thought was to form a small band of regular police. He organized, therefore, a few of the best of the old parish constables, paid them a regular wage, and set them to work.

There were at first seven of them, and they were not policemen as we know them, but detectives and "thief-takers." "Acting on information received, I proceeded to such-and-such a house, where I saw the accused." Such is the famous police formula even today; it was the duty of Fielding's detectives to secure the information, and to act upon it.

They were hated at first, because about the name "thief-taker" still hung the evil memory of Jonathan Wild and his betrayals. Later, this small band of detectives with their "robin redbreast" waistcoats and their badges of office—a tiny baton with a gilt crown on the top—became a national institution known as the Bow Street runners. The word "runner," by the way, did not mean that they always ran. It meant a scout or messenger. Before the days of the Bow Street runners, the same term was used for the look-out man at a gaming house, as well as for a sheriff's or prison officer.

The Bow Street runners were famous during the last years of the 18th century and the first of the 19th. We associate them with the Regency bucks, the bareknuckle prize-fighters and swashbuckling stage-coachmen.

There was Vickery, for instance, who secured information about a daring plan to rob the Central Post Office. He gave his information to the authorities, but they refused to believe him. Vickery went back to the underworld from which his information had come. He returned with a bunch of keys with which, before the astonished Post Office officials' eyes, he opened door after locked door of their stronghold, until he brought them to the room in which their money and valuables were. The intending robbers, Vickery said, had been there often, but had delayed their coup in the hope that they would in time secure a really big haul.

Another case of Vickery's became world-famous. Two men called at a jeweler's in the shadow of St. Paul's Cathedral, and asked the jeweler to show them his wares. The two "customers" delighted the jeweler by ordering £35,000 worth of jewelry, which was parceled up while the two men went away to make arrangements about paying for it. They did not return, and when the jeweler opened his parcel, it contained only rubbish. At some point in the proceedings the two men had exchanged their worthless parcel for the real one full of jewels.

Vickery traced the thieves to the continent, chased them through France, Holland and Germany, and returned £20,000 worth of the stolen jewels to the owner.

Perhaps the best example of hard, patient detective work by one of the runners is the story of Keys and the coiner, Jem Coleman. The police today often know a great deal about a criminal without being able to catch him and produce enough evidence to convict him. They must wait and watch patiently, until all the evidence is in their hands.

So it was with Coleman. The runners knew that he made counterfeit coins. They could at any time have laid their hands on the small fry who passed

Coleman's counterfeits for him. But it was Coleman himself they wanted, and Coleman was a shy bird. He lived in the basement of a house in a maze of narrow streets, no one knew quite where, and he came out only after he had made very sure that no one whom he did not know was in the street.

Keys of the Bow Street runners was put on Coleman's trail. He suspected where Coleman lived, and he hired a man to pass through the street daily, disguised as a milkman, with a yoke and a pair of pails on his shoulders, delivering milk. Every day for two months he went through the street, selling milk. Nothing happened until the day that Coleman peeped out of his hiding-place and saw no one in the street except the milkman who had been there every day for two months. Coleman left the house. The milkman took his news to Keys. At last the runners were sure where Coleman lived. That night they made a raid, capturing the counterfeiter himself and much of his equipment.

Coleman was hanged in due course, and a woman friend claimed his body; to bury it, she said. But she did not bury it, and the runners became inquisitive. They made another call. They found that she was still carrying on Coleman's work, hiding the counterfeiting molds in the coffin under the dead man's body.

The runners had to be brave, as well as intelligent and determined. Armstrong of Bow Street fought a running battle with a noted highwayman along the roofs of three houses in Chatham. The robber fired his pistol point-blank at Armstrong, missed, and they closed in a desperate wrestle. The robber tried to hurl himself and the detective into the street, but Armstrong hung on, and brought the highwayman triumphantly down to trial and execution.

Macmanus, a great fighter and, we may guess from his name, an Irishman, was set upon when unarmed and off duty by an armed gang determined to kill him. He fought them off, and though injured made his escape.

The Bow Street runners are replaced now by detective inspectors, sergeants and constables of the C.I.D., and by Scotland Yard's radio crime cars, still ready to go to the ends of the earth in pursuit of a suspect, still ready to close, though unarmed, with a desperate gunman.

Here is a story which shows that the methods used by Keys are used today. The C.I.D. wanted to catch a street bookmaker. They knew that he kept lookouts who would warn him instantly if any unknown or suspicious person entered the street. On a rainy day two of the C.I.D. men crept up on him with their knees bent, under cover of an umbrella, so that the bookmaker was deceived into thinking the two burly detectives were harmless children!

Another branch of the runners' work, the guardianship of royalty, is now carried on by "A" Division of the Metropolitan Police. We have a picture of

John Townsend, one of the most famous runners, who was attached to the Court to keep guard over King George IV. He was a smart little man, dressed in a light suit with knee-breeches, short gaiters, and a white hat with a great breadth of brim. He thought much of himself, and was careful to let people know that he was on intimate terms with royalty. He once refused to arrest a common tradesman, because the last two people he had arrested had been an earl and a marquis, and it would have lowered his reputation if he had had to deal with persons of lesser rank!

One day at a royal reception, a nobleman had the jeweled Order of the Garter cut from his very side. Townsend, who was at the reception, saw a man in court dress who looked as if he had no right in that distinguished assembly. But Townsend could not see the man's face, and he had to be very tactful, for not all King George IV's friends were quite respectable. Townsend therefore shadowed the man as he made his way through the palace rooms, among the glittering jewels and gleaming orders, until at last the suspect turned his head. Townsend, who knew every rogue in London, recognized him at once as a thief, searched him, found the Order, and carried off his captive to Bow Street.

The runners' pay was only 25s. a week, but in those days you could not call on the runners, as you can now call on the services of the C.I.D., without paying for them. Anyone who employed a runner on a case had to pay him a guinea a day, and 14s.

a day traveling expenses. Then, if he recovered your property, you were expected to pay him a substantial reward as well. There was a price of £40 on the head of any criminal wanted for a hanging offence.

It was said that the runners often refused to arrest a wanted man, though they knew well where to find him and could have secured a conviction, until he had committed that last fatal offence which made him worth £40 to them.

There were other ways of making money, not all of them honest. John Townsend, who left £20,000 when he died, was in the habit of warning rich and nervous ladies, wearing all their jewels on some special occasion, that there were rogues about, and they had better hand over their valuables to him for safekeeping. They did so, of course, and of course they gave old John a handsome present for taking such good care of them. Whether rogues were quite as plentiful as John Townsend liked to make out was another matter. When another famous runner died, leaving a sizeable fortune, a quantity of notes stolen years before from a Glasgow bank were said to have been found buried beneath his hearthstone.

Despite their faults, however, the runners did good work. But they were only a handful and the Horse Patrol, the only other organized police force in London, numbered but ten.

In 1780 the Gordon Riots broke out in London. They began as a protest against the repeal of certain anti-Catholic laws, but the rioters were soon joined by every rogue and vagabond from London's underworld. For six days the great city was defenceless while the mob burned and murdered and plundered. The outbreak could have been easily checked at the beginning by a handful of disciplined police properly controlled. But there was no such body. Only at the end of a week's terror were troops called in and the riot quelled at the cost of 200 people killed and 250 wounded by the troops' fire.

Thoughtful people began to wonder whether such a state of affairs must not be ended, but there was still the fear that a police force would be used by the government as a weapon against political opponents. So nothing was done, except that a night foot patrol of 68 armed men was established, to cover the roads on the outskirts of London to a distance of four miles from the "stones' ends"—the ends of the paved streets. In 1805 a new horse patrol was organized, and in 1806 Sir Robert Peel established the first day patrol for the West End of London, in three parties of eight men, each under an inspector. These patrols eventually reached a combined strength of 300 men.

Sixteen years later Peel, as Irish Secretary, reorganized the Royal Irish Constabulary. These were named "peelers," after him, and once more people began to ask whether such a force was not necessary for London also.

Times were changing. Government was no longer carried on by a handful of men at the whim of a king or queen, but by a cabinet of ministers answerable to its own party in Parliament, to an organized opposition, and, finally, to an increasing number of voters in the country. What was impossible and probably undesirable in 1729 was in 1829 an urgent necessity, and Peel carried his Metropolis Police Improvement Bill through both Houses of Parliament.

On the evening of September 29th, 1829, the first thousand of Peel's new police set out on patrol. They wore blue swallow-tail coats, rabbit-skin top hats covered with leather, Wellington boots of thick, unsupple leather, thick leather belts with 6-inch buckles which cut uncomfortably into their stomachs, and 4-inch deep leather stocks to make them keep their chins up. It was, according to one of them, a cross between the dress worn by the ex-Emperor Zoolooki of the Squeejee Islands, and the policeman in a pantomime.

They were assailed by the mob with shouts of "blue devils" and "the raw lobster gang." So high ran popular feeling against them that when a policeman was killed in quelling a riot, the coroner's jury returned a verdict of "justifiable homicide."

But Peel had been very careful in selecting his men. Many of them were former soldiers of exemplary character, and they were armed only with a truncheon. It was Peel's intention that the peace should be kept, whenever possible, by patience and good temper rather than by armed charges with cutlasses and pistols.

This has become a proud tradition of British police work. A party of distinguished continental visitors, shown around a mounted police depot in London, admired the polished saddles and the glittering equipment.

"But where," asked one of the visitors, "does the policeman keep his sabre and his rifle?"

"He doesn't have them," said their guide.

"Only this?" said the visitor wonderingly, fingering the long truncheon, or club, and thinking of continental riots with their bloodshed and rifle-shots and sabre-charges. "And does he find that enough?"

A mounted policeman stood near by. "Well, sir," he said, "I've been in the Mounted branch twenty-three years, and *I've* never had to use even my truncheon."

For the first ten years of the new police force's life, the Bow Street runners went on with their jobs. They generally took the jewel robberies, the rewards of which brought them money, and left murders and other unprofitable affairs to the "bobbies," as Sir Robert's men came to be called. All the murderers, it was noticed, were discovered; but very few of the jewel-robbers were. So the Bow Street runners had to go. If we ask of Bow Street's Robin Redbreasts "Who killed Cock Robin?" the answer is "I," said Robert Peel, "with my new police deal."

All the police in London, except the City of London force (which to this day remains independent), had come into the new organization. In 1839 the river police became the Thames Division of the Metropolitan Police. And in 1839 the Bow Street runners followed their last clue. Some of them hung on for a few years as private inquiry agents, but the new police were so much more efficient that, as the old runners faded away one by one, they were not replaced.

Their successors at Scotland Yard, headquarters of the new police, were two inspectors and six sergeants of a special detective branch formed in 1842. In 1878 the detective branch was enlarged, reorganized as the Criminal Investigation Department, and given its own Assistant Commissioner, a young barrister named Howard Vincent. We can see the new Department at work in a fascinating case which showed straightaway that though detection in storybooks may come from a flash of brilliant intuition, the real thing is more a matter of an infinite capacity for taking pains.

The "Rock" case began on the night of December 1st, 1882, when a young and newly married constable named Cole was patrolling his beat in London's East End. There was a thick fog, but about 10 o'clock he saw a man clambering over a low wall. Cole challenged the man, and as he did not stop, closed with him. The man pulled a gun and fired three shots, two of which missed and one of which hit the policeman. The shots attracted the attention of a young woman, who ran for help. Two other policemen came to the rescue, but Cole lay shot dead in the gutter, and the wanted man had vanished.

Left behind in his flight was a cabinetmaker's chisel with a blade 1¼-inches wide on which were a few scratches, unreadable to the naked eye, but showing under a magnifying glass the crudely scratched word "rock."

For a year the police worked on that slender clue, showing the chisel to every tool-maker, tool-seller and employer of cabinetmakers in the neighborhood. There were, as you may guess, hundreds of them. At last they came to an old woman who carried on her dead husband's business of sharpening chisels. She recognized the chisel, and declared that the scratches on it were made by herself and formed the word "Orrock," the name of a young desperado who had disappeared from his usual haunts shortly after the murder.

With a definite man to look for, the police soon found Mr. Orrock, who was doing a 12 months' sentence for burglary. Then they found his associates, who had a very shrewd idea what Orrock had been up to that foggy night. The police traced to him a hat left on the scene of the murder. Slowly, piece by piece, they built up their evidence, and Orrock was hanged.

Many a story-book detective, of course, would have done it in ten minutes, without leaving his armchair. In real life it is never as easy as that,

though as we shall see in a later chapter when we
watch the modern Scotland Yard at work detecting
the murderer of another police constable, it is none
the less sure.

4

The Man in Blue

THE ORGANIZATION OF THE UNIFORMED BRANCH
of the Metropolitan Police has changed little since
Sir Robert Peel's day. It is divided into four districts and 23 divisions. Each district has a Commander and Deputy Commander, and each division
is commanded by a Chief Superintendent. The divisions are further divided into sub-divisions, under a
Chief Inspector, the sub-divisions divided into station areas, and the station areas into beats and
patrols. Along the beat strides the man upon whom
the whole system depends, the uniformed police constable. Except for the very highest ranks of Scotland
Yard, every officer, every specialist of the C.I.D.,
the Thames Division, Mounted Branch and the rest,
must serve his time on the beat, and climb the ladder
of promotion rung by rung.

A hundred and twenty years ago, no training was
considered necessary for Sir Robert Peel's bobbies.
Then, in 1839, they were given a week's foot-drill
at Wellington Barracks. In those days the policeman

had only to think at the 2½ miles an hour of his majestic foot patrol. Now he has to think at 40, 50, 80 miles an hour in a fast and powerful car, handle radios and teleprinters, have some idea what clues may be useful to the laboratory scientists with his spectrograph, blood tests and ultra-violet ray lamp. So each recruit, on being accepted for the force, must spend a hard and concentrated 14 weeks at school.

There are two recruits' training schools. The older, founded in 1907, is at Peel House, not far from Scotland Yard. The other is at Hendon, in the northwestern suburbs, opposite the famous airfield, and has been used as a training school for recruits since 1946. The instruction at both schools is the same. The only difference is that there is no accommodation for policewomen at Hendon, and that Peel House, being in the heart of London, lacks Hendon's playing fields and its magnificent swimming pool. Nevertheless, the students at Peel House have time and opportunity for games, as do the students at Hendon. There are dances, concerts, film shows—and much hard work.

The policeman's "bible" is some 600 closely printed pages of the General Orders of the Metropolitan Police, and after his 14 weeks at school, the recruit is expected to know his way around this huge volume almost literally in his sleep. He must know—to take a few subjects at random—the law relating to performing animals and birds, what color a street messenger's licence is, how to handle any kind of traffic accident, what dodges street bookmakers get up to, what a counterfeit coin looks and feels like. So that he can look after himself and handle and disarm, if necessary, a truculent customer without hurting him too much, the police recruit is taught self-defense by experts of the Judo Club who are also members of the Metropolitan Police. He visits the Royal mews and sees all the Royal carriages and liveries, so that he can identify them on ceremonial occasions. He has to acquire a working knowledge of London and of the organizations which govern London.

There are realistic reconstructions of robberies, burglaries, murders, suicides, and street accidents to teach him what he must do when, as a patrolling constable, he is called to the scene of such crimes. He must learn first aid, in which every policeman is proficient and on which he is re-examined every three years of his service. He is encouraged to learn swimming and lifesaving. He learns how to sketch the scene of a crime or a traffic accident, and his observation is sharpened by an exercise such as this: making a mental note of all the objects on a tray, and naming them correctly some minutes after the tray has been removed. This is followed by many more detailed exercises in observation.

To broaden his mind, and encourage him to take a wider interest in life, he has classes in music appreciation and in art. He also learns some elementary science, to help him help Scotland Yard's laboratory.

He takes, in all, 232 subjects at the school, and is not considered to be a police constable until he has passed three examinations in them.

When the recruit has finished his course and passed his final examination at the Training School, he is posted to a division, where he will have his first real experience of police work. For a fortnight he attends the local magistrates' court; for another fortnight he walks a day beat with an experienced constable; then, still with an experienced man, he has a fortnight's night patrol. After that he is on his own, and that is a frightening moment. But he soon settles down to the interest of the job.

To the outsider, the "bobby" on his beat seems to lead a dull life. This is not so. Think of it in this way: every murderer, housebreaker, forger, criminal of any kind, has to pass at some time through those streets which the uniformed policeman is patrolling. Through those streets he has to take goods from where he has stolen them to where he will dispose of them. If he wants to get rid of the knife or revolver with which he has committed murder, he must bury it or throw it into the river on some policeman's beat. And that policeman has the chance of spotting him.

A uniformed constable late one night stopped a passer-by who was carrying an ordinary sports bag.

"What've you got there?" he asked.

"Just my tools, mate," said the man.

"Let's have a look," said the constable.

The bag was opened, and the policeman saw three pieces of wood, one on top of the other.

"And what might those be?" he asked.

"Just something I use at my job," said the man with the bag. "You see, I'm a carpenter."

The policeman knew little about carpentry, and the answer might easily have satisfied a man who thought beat-work dull. But this constable had developed a nose for crime. He fiddled for a few minutes with the three innocent-seeming pieces of wood. Suddenly they opened out in his hands into two very long pieces of wood. And these two long pieces of wood, with equal suddenness, came apart, and the constable found himself standing there with one of the neatest and most ingenious folding ladders Scotland Yard has ever seen.

"Oho," said the constable. "I think you'd better come along to the station and explain exactly what you're doing with *this*."

Then there was a policewoman once who was given an ordinary routine inquiry to follow up. It concerned a missing woman. Incidentally, dozens of people are reported to the police as missing every year. Some of these people are not "missing" at all. They have gone away for their own private reasons. The police spend much time and energy tracing them, with nothing to show at the end of it but a door slammed in their faces and an indignant invitation to mind their own business. So the policewoman made the usual routine inquiries in the usual routine way, except that nothing was routine to her, and nothing was uninteresting. When she had made her inquiries, which led her nowhere in particular, she went back to the police station and said, "I've absolutely nothing to go on, but I don't like this case. I think it may be a murder."

"All right," she was told. "You'd better tell the C.I.D. what you've got."

The policewoman told the C.I.D., and they took up the trail. Within a short time they had arrested a man for the murder of that missing woman, whose name was Mrs. Olive Durand-Deacon.

So you see there is nothing dull or routine about the policeman's beat. The constable on his beat is the foundation of the English police system. He seems to do little except walk about, stop a boy from kicking his football in the street, or tell a driver that he's parking his car where he has no right to park it. But if he were taken away, we would be back to the days of Jack Sheppard and the Gordon Riots.

So for a year every recruit, whether he is a future Commander of the C.I.D. or a Master of Arts of Cambridge University, goes out on the beat. He has to pass another examination after six months in his division, and a final probationary examination after 15 months' service. Toward the end of his probation, he spends a month on detachment with the C.I.D., a fortnight with the traffic patrol cars, a fortnight with the crime cars, a month on duty inside the police station, a fortnight at the magistrates' court, and a week with the river patrols of the Thames Division. If he can ride, he may spend a little time with the Mounted Branch.

All this gives him a working knowledge of the other branches with which he must co-operate, and it helps him make up his mind what he himself would like to do. He can either stay with the uniformed branch, or apply for one of the specialist branches. Many recruits want to join the C.I.D. When asked why, they mutter something about having read detective stories. The veterans of the C.I.D. smile a grim smile at that, because the real work of the C.I.D., as we shall see in later chapters, is generally very different from the work of the C.I.D. as shown in most detective stories.

5

The Brain at Work

As in all large and efficient organizations, every branch of the Metropolitan Police is convinced that it is the best, and that without its help every other department would be more helpless than a football player without any feet. This is as it should be, for it would be a poor and spiritless department which did not think well of itself. And of course it is true, for every department *is* the best—

at its particular job; and all the departments inter-
lock into a vast machine, one part of which cannot
work without the others.

Scotland Yard might have all the most brilliant
scientists in the world in its laboratory, performing
miracles of analysis with their arsenic tests and
plaster casts of footprints. But they would be quite
useless without the C.I.D. to bring them the clues
for analysis and to arrest the criminals. In turn, if
there were no uniformed policemen on the beat, the
C.I.D. would be in the position of the Bow Street
runners, able to detect only a fraction of crime. And
if there were no clerks to send the pay sheet out
to the divisional police station, the man on the beat
would get so disgusted that he would soon patrol
the beat no more.

So you must see the police organization as a
single machine, the brain of which is New Scotland
Yard. This does not mean that all the cleverest
policemen work there. But into New Scotland Yard
comes information from all over the world. From
New Scotland Yard goes information, or instructions, upon which criminals are arrested in Glasgow
or Greenwich or Grenoble. In other words, New
Scotland Yard is not only the headquarters of the
Metropolitan Police, but also a storage place of information upon which any police force, anywhere,
may draw. In the Central Office of the C.I.D. there
are detectives ready day and night to go to the
scene of an important crime anywhere in Great

Britain or even abroad if necessary. The Scientific Laboratory analyzes specimens sent from all police forces in the Home Counties. And the Detective Training School at Hendon, run by the C.I.D., trains detectives not only from the Metropolitan and some British provincial forces, but also from all over the Commonwealth.

Inside this brain work two thousand men and women, policemen and civilians. Into this brain come between two and three thousand telephone calls an hour, two or three thousand letters or documents a day, and Morse wireless signals in a dozen languages from all over Europe, as well as teleprinter bulletins from district and divisional headquarters.

Unless each of these messages is sent to its correct destination within the Yard, the brain cannot function. The Chief Superintendent of the Public Carriage Office would no doubt be interested to hear that a murder had been committed in Notting Hill. The Chief Superintendent of the Flying Squad would dance, perhaps with joy, if he received a complaint that tea in the canteen at Leman Street Section House was *still* being served too weak. But it wouldn't do. There must be a brain within a brain, to see that each message reaches, with the least possible delay, the one person of Scotland Yard's busy two thousand who is waiting to deal with it. That brain within the brain is the telephone switchboard and the Registry.

If you dial Whitehall 1212, you will be put through to the switchboard at New Scotland Yard. This switchboard carries about 50 outside lines, and another 32 connecting it directly with police stations and police boxes in the Metropolitan Police area. It has 1200 extensions to telephones inside New Scotland Yard, and it is the switchboard superintendent's proud boast that within five seconds of taking your call, one of her operators will have put you through to the person you want.

All the switchboard staff are civilians. So are the staff of the Registry, who receive, sort, register and distribute everything which comes into the Yard by post, as well as the contents of 31 twice-daily bags from districts and divisions.

Their work begins at 7:30 in the morning, when the mail arrives, and every letter must at once be sorted for urgency. It may be an anonymous piece of information about the murder Central Office is working on. It may be from the crackpot who writes every week from Canada to tell Scotland Yard sad stories of his persecution by persons unknown. It may be a request from a provincial or Continental force for information about the murky history of some rogue they have to present for trial in three or four days' time. Or it may be an application for the Metropolitan Police Central Band to play in the parks next summer.

Registry knows unfailingly how important each letter is, and who will deal with it. It will be given a reference number. If there is already a file on that particular subject, it will be attached to that file. If not, a new file will be opened for it. Registry knows exactly who, in that vast building, has each file. And before the letter leaves Registry, a note will be made of its contents and sender for entering in the main index. By nine o'clock—earlier if it is top priority of urgency—the letter will be on someone's desk, ready to be dealt with.

There are 1½ million cards in Registry's main index, arranged alphabetically. Anyone who has written to the Yard, been written about to the Yard, or come within the knowledge of the Yard, criminally or otherwise, is docketed away there. Officers in the divisions have instructions to 'phone about any case they may be working on, to see if Registry knows anything helpful. Registry takes between 100 and 150 phone calls a day in this way alone.

And upstairs, row upon row, are the 1½ million files to which the main index refers. Here is the history of Scotland Yard—murders and frauds and robberies and complaints and requests for the band and anonymous letters from crackpots and letters about pedlars' licences and the road-worthiness of taxicabs. Here are two traitors, Klaus Fuchs and Neville Heath. And here too is Bill Jones, who thought the police ought to have something better to do than stop him parking his car in Parliament Square. And here is Anon, who returned a watch and purse illicitly acquired, together with a small sum of conscience money. Here is last year's murderer who thinks, because his crime has been forgotten by the public, he has got away with it. But Scotland Yard doesn't forget. There's his file, a little dusty perhaps, but waiting . . . waiting for that tiny addition which may come any day, any year, and which will hang him at last.

From Registry the messengers pad silently, endlessly, with their files down the long corridors to the Yard's various departments. "A" for Administration deals with complaints, donations to police charities, fortune telling, movements of Royalty, ceremonial functions, decorations and awards, the telephone box system, shorthand tests, discipline, the Mounted Branch, and the women police. "B" for Traffic and Transport runs the Public Carriage Office, the Lost Property Office, examines the causes of accidents, arranges parking places, and sees in general that London does not strangle itself utterly in the noose of its huge traffic problem. "C" is for Criminal Investigation—and we will investigate them later. "D" is for Organization—clothing and appointments, recruiting, first aid, buildings, furniture, equipment, medical services, communications and training. Each of these four has an Assistant Commissioner in command. "S" Department is the Secretariat which owns, among many other things, the Registry, the Aliens Registration Offices and the Press and Information Department. At its head is the Secretary of the Office of the Commissioner of Police of the

Metropolis. The sixth department, "L," is the Legal Department, directed by the Solicitor to the Commissioner of Police of the Metropolis.

At the head of the force is the Commissioner, with a Deputy Commissioner as his first lieutenant. In the past many Commissioners have been distinguished military men. Field Marshal Lord Byng of Vimy, a famous general of the First World War, took office in 1928, and was succeeded by the no less famous Marshal of the Royal Air Force Lord Trenchard, who made many reforms in the police organization. The present Commissioner, Sir Harold Scott, who took office in 1945, is a former civil servant. He is a quiet, bespectacled man who gives no outer indication of the qualities needed in a successful "thief-taker." Nevertheless, Sir Harold Scott faced the post-war crime wave of black-marketeers and service deserters with courage, persistence and unflurried confidence. What is more, with the help of the machine which he controls, he has beaten it.

But when you think of New Scotland Yard, you must think not of the Commissioner or Assistant Commissioners or the head of the Finger Print Branch or the Flying Squad. These are important, but the machine is more important. And the machine is a team of 20,000 men and women, police officers in uniform and plain clothes, clerks and secretaries and van drivers and biologists and wireless experts and motor mechanics and canteen assistants. Most of their names are unknown. But their work is not unknown. Because of them, more than eight million people can go safely about their work and their play, and sleep peacefully in their beds every night, with little fear of a modern Jack Sheppard or Jonathan Wild.

6

Criminal Records

THE TELEPHONE RANG ONE NIGHT ON THE GRAY-haired sergeant's desk.

"Hallo, my old Sherlock Holmes," said the jovial voice of the Chief Inspector C.I.D. at the other end. "I've got a sticky little murder here in Soho. I'm sending three witnesses up to look through your photograph albums. I don't think there's a hope they'll identify anyone; they only just glimpsed a man in a dim light on the stairs."

An hour or two later the sergeant rang up the Chief Inspector, and gave a name, a description and an address.

As the sergeant traveled home, the inspector was knocking like fate on the murderer's door. . . .

They call it at the Yard "Catching criminals on paper," and it is done by the Criminal Record Office of the C.I.D.

We have yet to see the C.I.D. at work but this is the place to learn about its Record Office.

The Criminal Record Office, though staffed by Metropolitan Police and housed at Scotland Yard, is national in character. It contains complete records of all persons convicted of crime in the United Kingdom, and provides information for police forces all over England, Wales and Scotland. Most countries have some centralized system or systems of criminal records, and C.R.O. is in direct touch with these national offices all over the world. Thus it is both a national and an international registry of crimes, a "Who's who" of their perpetrators, a means of enabling new crimes to be traced to old criminals, several crimes traced to the same person, and old criminals to be recognized with certainty when they are re-arrested.

C.R.O.'s registers of persons convicted of any crime of real importance are kept complete by information which prison wardens are required by law to supply, but a great deal of information about such persons can be supplied only by the police through whose hands they pass. You will see, for instance, when we come in a later chapter to the Antiquis case, how vital a part was played in the murderer's arrest by the information C.R.O. could supply about one man's associates.

The central registry contains such information as the criminal's name, date and place of birth, description, distinctive peculiarities, photographs, and particulars of conviction and imprisonment.

Each file is given a number based on the year in

which it is opened, and the number of files opened in that year. Thus, C.R.O. No. 5461 /51 would be the 5461st C.R.O. file opened in 1951. That C.R.O. number identifies that offender for all time, and forms the basis of the wonders which C.R.O. performs daily.

It may startle you a little to learn that between forty and fifty thousand new ones are opened every year.

You must understand, of course, that if a file is opened for a man upon his first arrest, and his photograph and fingerprints taken, file, photograph and fingerprints are all immediately destroyed if he is acquitted at his trial. C.R.O. is concerned only with *convicted* persons.

Based upon this central registry is the Crime Index. Criminals are rather unimaginative persons. They sometimes stick to much the same kind of crime, and commit it in much the same kind of way. It is very rare—to take an extreme instance—for a pickpocket to turn burglar. And a housebreaker who has turned a dishonest penny for years by breaking windows with treacle and brown paper does not often abandon his old method in favor of a jemmy, the common name for a short crowbar.

The good local C.I.D. man knows the peculiarities of his local criminals. When a new crime comes to his notice, he can say immediately, "Hallo, that looks like Bill Jones's work." He would know that Bill Jones had an address in Waterlow Street, or frequented a certain public house with Big Georgie Smith and Tiny Brown. He would drop in to see Bill Jones and his friends, and ask Bill Jones to account for his movements on such and such a night.

But supposing Bill Jones did a job one week in Wapping and next week in Wimbledon? Suppose the week after that he took a day excursion ticket to Winchester, and in a month's time was busily thieving away in Wales? There would always be the same signs of Bill Jones's handiwork, but to the police in Wapping and Wimbledon and Winchester and Wales it would mean nothing. They wouldn't know Bill Jones's characteristics, nor his name, nor his address, nor where he drank his pint of beer, nor who his friends were. He would be just a shadow, and shadows are very, very difficult to catch.

So in 1913 Scotland Yard set to work systematically to build a Crime Index, in which all the information about Bill Jones could be easily found and made available to police forces anywhere. The Crime Index is in fact several indexes. There is the Method Index, the Wanted Index, the Nominal Index, the Cheque Index, and various photograph albums and photo sheets, each of which we will look at in turn.

Take first the Method Index. In the nominal section are 2¾ million names, not of separate people, but of habitual criminals, each with his C.R.O. number, and each perhaps using several aliases. There is, for instance, one woman who has used over two hundred aliases, and one man with 440! There is a

separate card for each of these aliases—but only one
C.R.O. number; so that Bill Jones may be wanted
in Wapping as Tom Smith and at Winchester as
Harry Brown, but an inquiry about either of these
will inevitably lead, because of the C.R.O. number, to Bill Jones, and Bill Jones's associates, and
Bill Jones's address.

There is also on each card in the nominal section
a reference to the Main Card of the Method Index,
and on these Main Cards are recorded the actual
methods used by criminals.

These cards are classified according to the crime,
and the catalogue of these classifications occupies, in
Scotland Yard's own book about the C.R.O., no
fewer than 16 pages. Under "Breakings," for instance, there are separate categories for breaking
into churches, breaking into movies, breaking into
garages, offices, pavilions, safes, schools, shops or
workshops, warehouses. And "breaking into houses"
will be further sub-divided into the method of making the entry—such as climbing, going through the
rear or the window or over the roof—the *kind* of
house entered, the time.

Now let us suppose that a person calling himself Harry Brown gets acquainted with a servant in
a large country house near Winchester one Saturday evening, persuades her to give him a meal in
the kitchen, and while she is engaged upstairs, has
a quick look around and gets away with the silver.

The case is reported to the police. There will be

a telephone call to C.R.O.—there are in fact about 160,000 calls a year—asking for any information about Harry Brown.

C.R.O. will look first in the nominal section under the name Harry Brown. There will probably be some hundreds of Harry Browns, one of which may be an alias of the policeman's old friend, Bill Jones. But that is not enough. So C.R.O. will look at the section of the Method Index dealing with house-breaking. They will look under the sub-heading "Artifice used—servant, making acquaintance of." They will find that this is a favorite trick of a number of criminals using the alias "Harry Brown," including Bill Jones. Still not enough. They will look under the sub-heading "Premises entered—country mansion." Aha, not many criminals using the alias Harry Brown and scraping acquaintance with servants are fond of country mansions. But Bill Jones is. Still not quite enough, however. So C.R.O. looks under "Time entered—week end," and finds that Bill Jones *alias* Harry Brown always gets up to his tricks on Saturday evenings. They haven't proved, of course, that Bill Jones did the job. But they have given the local C.I.D. enough material to justify asking Bill Jones a lot of very personal questions.

There are, however, more pieces of helpful evidence. Bill Jones may have an unconscious trick of scratching the back of his head while he is talking. That trick will be filed away on a card in the section devoted to Characteristic Peculiarities. The servant at the Winchester mansion may never have heard Bill Jones's name, but she did notice this scratching of the head. Well, there it is, with Bill Jones's C.R.O. number against it. She may have noticed that he had three gold-filled teeth, or a twitching mouth. There they are, filed in the Deformities section—still against Bill Jones's number. She may have noticed a tattoo mark. C.R.O. has a section of tattoo marks. Bill Jones may have told her that his friends always called him "Fido." C.R.O. has a section of nicknames. And so on through the "Miscellaneous" section recording the peculiarities of persons who before their conviction were barbers or clergymen or doctors or policemen.

There is one further section—the "Dead" section. This does not mean that Bill Jones is filed there when he passes away. It only means that he is dead to the police, for his card is put there when he has been convicted and safely locked away in prison for a term longer than six months.

So much for the Method Index, with its many thousands of cards.

There is also a Wanted Index, containing the names and methods of all persons reported as wanted for serious offences. It is compiled from information supplied not only by the Metropolitan Police, but by forces all over the country as well.

Persons are recorded in this index whether they are known to have a criminal record or not, and whether their identity is known or not. Therefore if "A Man" is circulated as wanted, and a description is given, he goes down in the index, together with brief details of his offence; until there comes another report of "A Man" committing the same sort of crime in the same sort of way and answering the same sort of description. Presently "A Man" begins to acquire a name and a method and a personality. He was housebreaking in Halifax one week, in Huddersfield the week before. It looks as if he's working the Yorkshire towns. Someone in C.R.O. will get on the telephone to the Yorkshire police, and "A Man" will find a policeman on the beat scanning him with an eagle eye and asking him what he's carrying in that little black bag.

Then there is the Cheque Index. Here are recorded particulars of cheques, or books of cheques, reported missing. It is used to connect up criminals with a series of cheque offences, and to assist in establishing the identity of persons handling these cheques.

Finally there are the photograph albums, and the photo sheets.

The photograph albums contain photographs, arranged under classifications of crime, of the most important persons recorded in the Method Index, and particularly those who operate in London or the surrounding districts. Witnesses are sent up to C.R.O. by the C.I.D. to see if they can identify someone from these albums.

The photo sheets are used to compile registers

maintained at each Metropolitan Police station and containing particulars of active criminals who are known to operate in, live in or frequent the subdivisions or sections concerned. Each consists of a form giving photograph and personal particulars, which are kept up to date by an exchange of information between C.R.O. and the police station.

Now this vast amount of information controlled by the Chief Superintendent and men of C.R.O. would be quite useless unless it could be got out quickly to the men on the beat and in divisional C.I.D. in London and provincial forces.

Much of it goes out in C.R.O. publications, including the daily *Police Gazette*, which is circulated to every police force in the country. Periodical supplements concerning particular crimes and criminals are also issued.

Then there are the requests for information from Metropolitan and provincial forces. Sometimes the information can be given very quickly, and will concern only one criminal. Sometimes there has to be a long search of the various indexes, and C.R.O. will submit a list of 30 or 40 criminals who *may* fill the bill.

How important these inquiries are you may judge from a couple of murder cases. Case Number One was "A Man" who was murdering women in the West End of London. No name, no description, only a method. C.R.O. could not help, and the

C.I.D. had to look among London's eight millions for "A Man." They got him, but it was a long job. Case Number Two began with a telephone query to know if C.R.O. had anything on a Colonel Heath. C.R.O. had. They had his photograph, his particulars, his past history, his associates. The police were at once looking for a particular person with a name, a description and photograph which could be circulated all over the country. It was circulated, and a smart young C.I.D. man led Scotland Yard to the arrest of the murderer Neville Heath.

Last but not least in the ways of putting C.R.O.'s information at the disposal of the police are the men of C.R.O. themselves.

When you go into the long room in which the various indexes are housed, you will see these men, perhaps in little groups, chatting together. They are not chatting about the weather, or last week's football match. One of them has noticed some little peculiarity in a case which has reminded him of something else. "I say, Bill, doesn't this put you in mind of that Thetford fellow. . . ." They discuss it, other experts join them, they begin looking up cards, and presently there is a telephone call to warn some local force that Bill Jones, description and peculiarities given, *may* be paying them a visit in the near future.

Some of these men have been working in C.R.O. for over 20 years, and as soon as a crime is reported, can name offhand, without looking at the index, two or three likely suspects. The Chief Superintendent's "Brains Trust" consists of four such experienced officers with a century of police service between them.

Now let us go back to the beginning of the chapter, and fill in the gaps of that midnight telephone call to one of C.R.O.'s most experienced sergeants.

A girl murdered in Soho. The girl's sister, the sister's husband and a friend had been going up to her flat, and had passed in the dim light on the stairs a man who said in a muffled voice, "She isn't in." Nothing more than that to work on.

The three witnesses were sent up in charge of a C.I.D. aid to look through C.R.O.'s photograph albums, in the hope that they might be able to identify someone. They couldn't. But the gray-haired sergeant didn't give up.

"Now just tell me," he said to the murdered girl's sister, "everything you possibly can about the incident. Was he a short man or a tall man? Was he dark or fair?"

She didn't know, she hadn't noticed.

"What exactly did he say?"

"He just said, 'She isn't in.' Oh!" The weary, distraught girl suddenly sat upright as she remembered something. "He spoke in a funny voice."

"What sort of a funny voice?" asked the sergeant patiently. "Was it an accent? Welsh? Scottish? North Country?"

"No, it was just funny, as if there was something wrong with his mouth."

"Wait there a moment, please," said the sergeant.

He went into the big room, to the Speech subsection of the Deformities section of the Crime Index. Carefully he turned over the cards. There was a man with a cleft palate who had once climbed in through the window of a hospital and tried to stab a nurse.

The sergeant found a photograph of this man, mixed it with other photographs of similar men.

"Now," he said to the girl. "Close your eyes. Try to remember the man you saw on the staircase. Now open your eyes. Can you see anyone here?"

"That's him," she said unhesitatingly, pointing to the man with the cleft palate.

Luck? Or the skill of a brilliant organization?

7

Fifty Years of Fingerprints

AT ABOUT HALF-PAST SEVEN ON THE MORNING of Monday, March 27th, 1905, a painter waiting for a friend opposite Chapman's Oil Shop in High Street, Deptford, South London, saw an old gentleman come to the door of the shop with blood on his face, shirt and hands. The old gentleman stared

In constant touch with the police all over London: New Scotland Yard, headquarters of the Metropolitan Police, as it is today.

Scotland Yard's First Detective. John Townsend, a famous Bow Street runner. The runners, or "Robin Redbreasts"—so called because of their scarlet waistcoats—formed London's first band of organized, regular police.

The Bow Street runners were replaced by a police force which was popularly known as the "peelers," after their founder, Sir Robert Peel. This illustration shows one of the first "peelers," in 1829.

"Catching criminals on paper." This is the work done by the Criminal Record Office of the Criminal Investigation Department. It is in Scotland Yard but it is a file available for all Britain and a large part of the world as well.

Criminals generally, but not always, work to pattern. Those who regularly use a ladder or a rope or a bicycle, for example, find their habits recorded at the Yard. And if they have been tattooed or are deformed, that is classified, too . . . The ladder, the rope, the tattoo, the bicycle . . . they may lead to another arrest and another conviction.

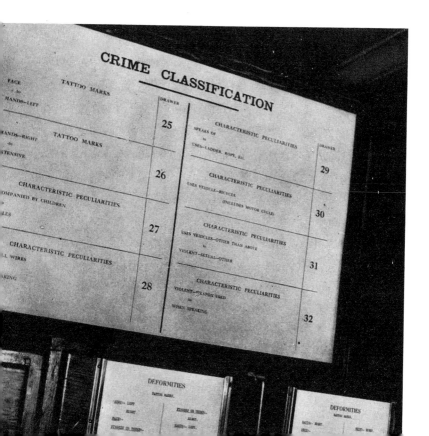

Tom Smith, a well-known London policeman in the eighteen fifties.

In contrast to the photograph on the preceding page, this picture shows a modern police constable with his comfortable, well-fitted tunic, collar and tie.

First lesson in fingerprints. Detectives from many parts of the world come to Scotland Yard's finger-print school.

Chief Superintendent Cherrill checks over his Scene of Crime box. It contains complete equipment for testing and recording fingerprints and impressions at the scene of the crime (Right).

A sectional map of an area in London with discs showing the disposition of police radio cars (Lower Right).

Fingerprints are sent to Scotland Yard's print library from all over Britain and from many parts of the world for possible identification.

All tasks come alike to the River Police, many of whom have served in the Royal Navy and the Merchant Navy.

about him for a few moments in a vacant kind of way, then disappeared, closing the door behind him.

The painter looked up and down the street for a policeman, couldn't see one—and coolly went off to catch his train! An hour later the police were called to that shop. They found the old gentleman, whose name was Farrow, and who was the shop manager, lying dead across the fender of the downstairs kitchen with appalling injuries to his head, caused by some such heavy blunt instrument as a jemmy. Upstairs they found Mrs. Farrow, similarly injured, but still alive. She died in the hospital a few days later, without having been able to make a statement.

It was Mr. Farrow's custom to hand over the week's takings of the shop to the owner every Monday morning. When the police looked for this money—which was generally about £13—they found nothing but six-pence and a penny on the bedroom floor where Mrs. Farrow had been assaulted. They also found a rifled cash box.

On the black enameled tray of this cash box was a single blurred fingerprint. This was the first fingerprint, under the new system introduced at Scotland Yard in 1901, to be used as vital evidence in a murder trial.

Fingerprints had been used by Scotland Yard since 1895, but it was not until Mr. E. R. Henry, later Sir Edward Henry, who had studied fingerprints in India, became Assistant Commissioner of the C.I.D. in 1901 that fingerprinting was recognized as an infallible method of identification. At the time of the Deptford murders, there were between 80,000 and 90,000 sets of fingerprints at the Yard, which meant between 800,000 and 900,000 prints of separate fingers. There are now about 1½ million sets, and we will see how these are used in a moment, when we have finished with the Deptford murders.

Inquiries into the deaths of Mr. Farrow and his wife led the police to two brothers named Stratton, who were known to the police. Several witnesses had seen two men in the neighborhood of Chapman's Oil Shop at about seven o'clock that morning, but identification of the Stratton brothers was by no means certain.

When the Strattons were arrested, however, their fingerprints had been taken, and there was a breathless hush in court when Inspector Collins, a fingerprint expert from New Scotland Yard, was called to give evidence.

He said that he had had ten years' experience of fingerprints, and never in that time had he found two fingerprints alike. The highest number of points to agree in the fingerprints of different persons was three. The fingerprint on the tray of the cash box, he said, was identical in 12 points with the print taken of Alfred Stratton's right thumb, and as an expert he was prepared to swear that the print on the tray was Alfred Stratton's beyond shadow of a doubt.

The honest British jurymen looked perplexedly at the strange photographs of loops and whorls handed up to them. The print on the tray was blurred, while the print taken from Alfred Stratton was very clear. Why was that, they asked Inspector Collins. The inspector explained that the clearness of the print depended on the pressure of the finger. If the jury liked, he would demonstrate. He went to the jury box, and took impressions of one juryman's thumb, to show the difference in clearness between light and strong pressures. He went on to point out in detail the similarities in the two photographs.

Inspector Collins and his new and wonderful fingerprints were discussed that night in many thousands of homes. Some people said it was all nonsense. More sensible people waited for the second day of the trial, to see what was going to happen.

The defence called an expert who was prepared to swear that the whole of Scotland Yard's new fingerprint system was erroneous. The judge, in his summing up, said, "If it is correct that people's hands and fingers vary so much, there is, at any rate, an extraordinary amount of resemblance between the two marks we have seen, and therefore to a certain extent they are corroborative evidence in regard to Alfred. But," he added, "I do not think you, gentlemen of the jury, would like to act upon those marks alone."

The jury retired to consider their verdict at 7:45 that night. At ten minutes past 10, they filed back into the jury box. There was a breathless silence in the packed court when the foreman rose to his feet. He announced a verdict of "Guilty" against Alfred and Albert Stratton. They were the first murderers to be hanged on a fingerprint, for though there was a strong presumption in the rest of the evidence that the Strattons were guilty, there can be no doubt that, in spite of the judge's cool summing up, the jury was finally persuaded by the evidence of Inspector Collins.

As recently as 1908, a judge and jury disagreed even more strongly about the value of fingerprint evidence. An offender at Birmingham had left the imprint of one or more of his fingers on a champagne bottle. The judge twice invited the jury to say they were not satisfied with the evidence of identity given by the fingerprint expert from Scotland Yard, and twice the jury refused to take the judge's advice, finding the accused man guilty.

In the years since those cases, judges, juries, criminals and Scotland Yard have learned much about fingerprints. Judges no longer hesitate to accept the scientifically established fact that no two people's prints—indeed, no two fingers of any one person's hand—are identical.

But how is this established fact used in catching criminals? The palm of the hand and the sole of the foot are marked by numerous lines or furrows which, with the ridges between, show many varieties of pattern, both in their general form and the finer details. Sir Francis Galton, the great British scientist, proved that these ridges and furrows remain unaltered in pattern from babyhood until death.

Fingerprints had been used in the East for untold years, in place of signatures on business documents, and while he was serving as Inspector-General of Police in Bengal, Mr. E. R. Henry, as he was known then, devised a system of classifying these patterns under four main types, known as loops, arches, whorls and composites. He then broke down these four types into sub-classifications according to the number of ridges and various finer details in the ridge characteristics.

In July, 1901, Mr. Henry introduced this system of classification at Scotland Yard. The fingerprints filed there according to Sir Edward Henry's classification are those of all persons who have been convicted and sentenced in Great Britain to imprisonment for serious criminal offences. A criminal's fingerprints form the basis on which is built up his personal file, and by this system of classification, fingerprints sent to the Yard can be matched against fingerprints in the files in a matter of minutes.

Let us take the case of a man charged at Cardiff with housebreaking and theft under the name of

John Smith. He is convicted, and sent to prison, where his fingerprints are taken by a prison officer. The fingers are not just pressed on to the stiff paper slip, but are rolled from side to side, so that there is a clear impression of each from nail-edge to nail-edge. On the back of the slip is recorded the prisoner's name, with dates and full particulars of the case. The slip is then sent to Scotland Yard, classified by one officer, checked by another so that there can be no possibility of mistake, and filed in its proper cabinet. To guard still further against mistakes of classification, the whole record is systematically examined from time to time.

After two years, say, Scotland Yard receives from the police or warden of a prison a slip containing the prints of a man on trial for theft, who has given the name of William Jones. Is anything known against him?

On receiving this slip, one fingerprint officer draws up the search form containing the full classification of the new prints, hands this slip over to another officer, who checks it, then looks under the appropriate classification in the file. Yes, identical prints are there—not in the name of William Jones, but of John Smith. And when "William Jones" comes into court and is convicted of the new offence, all the sins John Smith has committed in the past will be put in evidence against him when the time comes for judge or magistrate to ask about his criminal record.

Under Sir Edward Henry's system, fingerprints are classified according to the characteristics revealed by the entire set of fingers and thumbs together. This system works perfectly when there is a set of prints to be matched against a set of prints. But very often Scotland Yard will not be sent a full set of prints. There may be only a single blurred print, found on a broken window perhaps, or on a cash box. It would obviously take a very long time to find the match for this single print in the massive collection.

To overcome this difficulty, Superintendent Battley, head of the Finger Print Department at Scotland Yard in the 1920's, devised a method of classifying single fingerprints. The new system adopted, as the basis of classification, points of resemblance, not of sets, but of single prints. By its means any fingermark found at the scene of a crime can, unless hopelessly blurred, be readily classified and identified with any recorded print of the same finger in the Single Print Collection. This collection, by the way, contains only the prints of criminals convicted of offences belonging to the "breaking and entering" class, or thought likely to join that band.

There is one further collection of prints in the Finger Print Branch—the Scenes of Crime collection. Here are filed prints found at the scene of a crime which cannot be matched against prints already held by the Yard. This is how it works: a few years ago, a house was burgled at Watford, in Hertfordshire. The print of a right forefinger, believed to belong to the burglar, was found on a wine glass and sent to Finger Print Branch. A search was made, but that identical print was not in the records; in other words, that particular criminal had never before had his fingerprints taken and filed at the Yard. But the print from the wine glass was not forgotten. It was filed away for future reference. There were more burglaries, in Gloucestershire, Hertfordshire, Warwickshire, Leicestershire, Hertfordshire again; more fingerprints; and in each case experts were fairly certain that all these prints belonged to the man who had burgled that house at Watford. Well, twelve months after that first burglary, a man was arrested at Hitchin, his prints were taken, sent up to the Yard, and all the prints found at the scenes of those previous crimes could be identified as his. When he came into court, he had to face punishment not just for the Hitchin burglary for which he had been arrested, but all the rest of the series; and when he saw the fingerprint evidence against him, he admitted the lot.

"Latent" fingerprints—that is, prints visible only under a strong magnifying glass—can be developed with the aid of certain powders. Marks on knife blades, for instance, or on dark surfaces generally, are developed with "Gray" powder, a mixture of mercury and chalk. If the mark is on paper or other light surface, graphite or lamp black is used.

The powder is put on sparingly with an insufflator or a fine camel hair brush, the surplus blown away, and there is the print outline. Fingerprint experts don't like using powder if they can help it, for it sometimes obscures some characteristic detail. Now, with the aid of powerful angled lamps, cameras and projectors for showing up, photographing and enlarging latent prints, there are very few prints indeed which the experts cannot prepare for identification somehow or other.

The "Scene of Crime" boxes, which are kept packed and ready for immediate use by the fingerprint experts, contain everything needed for dealing with prints at the scene of a crime. There are graphite and gray powder, a magnifying glass, insufflator, tweezers for picking up delicate objects, a tape measure, probe, screwdriver, envelopes for exhibits, labels and other useful things. The famous Murder Bags, used by Scotland Yard and divisional C.I.D. men, similarly contain everything useful to a detective at the scene of a crime: small boxes for bullets, test tubes, cellophane wrappers for articles of clothing, and the like. These boxes and bags are fully stocked, and the man called to a case can pick them up from their shelf, and be on his way.

Now let us accompany the head of the Finger Print Branch, a Chief Superintendent, to the scene of a crime. He has picked up his Scene of Crime box, and is on his way to the house in which an old lady has been murdered in Berkshire. It is a big house with 22 rooms. The rooms are in a state of incredible confusion, partly no doubt because the murderer has ransacked the place for money or jewelry, but partly because the old lady has lived alone for many years, and accumulated in her rooms a strange jumble of clothes and boxes and garden implements and old rubbish.

Where, amid that confusion, does one begin looking for fingerprints? The Chief Superintendent says that he knows, within a few seconds of entering a room, whether he is going to be successful or not. He enters the room, stands there for a few minutes weighing the scene, getting the "feel" of it, reconstructing in his own mind what has probably happened. There has been a robbery. Therefore the criminal will have looked in certain places, opened certain boxes, to look for valuables. Some places in the room still have over them a film of undisturbed dust. So the murderer has not been there. Over other things are almost invisible threads of spiders' webs. No use looking there.

The Chief Superintendent narrows down the area of his search, and then goes to work. He knows that fingerprints are made by the emission of sweat or grease from the pores which increases, it has been said, because of the criminal's uncontrollable nervous excitement as he commits his crime. There are some objects which "take" prints very clearly— light surfaces, for example, such as glass and silver. On the dark surface of a rough iron grate, the print will still be there, it can be developed and photographed, but it is not as immediately clear. So the Chief Superintendent tries to think himself into the criminal's mind in this chaotic room, and to examine the things the criminal will have examined. Slowly, methodically, with his magnifying glass, he goes from object to object. Nothing is left out. There are many fingerprints which he can tell, by comparison with prints he has already taken, are those of the murdered woman. There are no others. That in itself is suspicious, denoting an old offender whose prints are already at Scotland Yard, and who has taken precautions to leave no prints this time. But however expert the criminal, he *always* leaves some trace. Whether that trace can be found or not, or turned into evidence for a court of law, is of course another matter. But there always *is* a trace, and Scotland Yard generally finds it.

This time there is a trace, a fingerprint. The criminal has been careful, but not quite careful enough. Something white on the floor has caught the Chief Superintendent's eye. He examines it carefully. It is the lid of a small cardboard box, of the kind used for jewelry. It has been thrown on the floor, trodden on and flattened. But it holds a single partial fingerprint, as if a man had picked it up gingerly between thumb and index finger.

The Chief Superintendent has found what he was looking for. Back goes the box to Scotland Yard. Is there an identical print in the collection? There is. It belongs to George Russell, a laborer and jobbing gardener, who has been convicted in the past of housebreaking. Scotland Yard has his full description. Out it goes to every police force and police station in the country. No one can evade that terrible net. Five days after the murder was discovered, George Russell is found at St. Albans, arrested and charged.

There is other evidence against him at the trial, but as in the case of the Stratton brothers, it is not conclusive. The fingerprint is the evidence on which George Russell will or will not hang. Forty-five years ago the judge might have hesitated to accept that evidence; but not today. The defence subjects the Chief Superintendent to a searching cross-examination, but he cannot be shaken. The print is Russell's. It can be nobody but Russell's. And George Russell is found guilty.

8

Crime and the Camera

PHOTOGRAPHY WAS USED LONG BEFORE FINGER-prints as a means of identifying criminals, and the camera is still one of science's greatest contributions to modern crime detection.

But the camera is not your old box Brownie. The Chief Inspector who is camera king of the

Finger Print Branch has all kinds of cameras at his command, from the neat little one which carries its own light, is loaded with 12 slides and can be carried by hand to photograph fingerprints at the scene of a crime, to giants used for photostating a dozen copies or so of each of a thousand documents needed in some complicated fraud case.

The Chief Inspector is a friendly, jolly, gentle man who devotes all the energy left over from his cameras to work for the Boy Scouts. But if you want to see him really lyrical you must watch him demonstrating the wonders of ultra-violet and infra-red photography, high pressure mercury lamps for spotlighting a tricky fingerprint, and other gadgets for revealing all kinds of things which the criminal would much rather keep wrapped in mystery.

Take fingerprints first. There is the common or garden fingerprint planted firmly on a good surface, and providing no trouble for anyone except the chap foolish enough to leave it behind him. But the criminal is rarely so obliging as that. He may have left nothing more than a minute deposit of sweat, almost invisible to the naked eye. But that can be brilliantly spotlit and photographed from such an angle that it will stand out from its background and reveal every turn of the telltale pattern of loops and whorls.

The same kind of spotlighting is used to make enlarged photographs of, for example, jemmy marks on a door or window frame. These show the ridges and indentations of the metal so closely that the tool itself can afterwards be identified from them as certainly as can a man from his fingerprints.

When a thief steals a car to sell it, his first action will be to remove the number stamped on the cylinder block. The Photographic Section can subject that erased number to a heat and chemical process, and photograph it so that despite the thief's hardest efforts it becomes readable again.

Then there are ultra-violet and infra-red photography. As you probably know, ultra-violet and infrared rays are at opposite ends of the spectrum, normally invisible, and there is a difference between the reflection or absorption of these rays and of "ordinary" light. The ultra-violet lamp, which you will meet again in the Science Laboratory, causes objects in its light to fluoresce—that is, to throw back and make visible the ultra-violet rays. Infrared rays have the power to penetrate anything opaque, such as a coat of paint, dirt, oil, or grease, and reveal what is underneath.

Moreover, things revealed by the ultra-violet and infra-red lamps can be photographed, although they are invisible to the ordinary eye, and those photographs can be produced as evidence in court to confound clever criminals who thought they had covered all their traces.

Let us look first under the u.v. lamp. Here is an identity card. The name is quite clearly written in ink—Thomas Walter Jones. But put it under the lamp and see what happens. Thomas Walter Jones disappears, and in his place is James Frederick Smith, the original owner of the identity card, whose name has been erased—as some criminal hoped!—and a fresh name written on top.

Here is a will, in which grandpa's fortune is clearly left to his affectionate grandson. Put it under the u.v. lamp, and you will see that there is no mention of the grandson. What grandpa *originally* wrote was "The Battersea Dogs' Home" which some criminally minded person—it couldn't possibly be the grandson, could it?—has rubbed out, and covered with grandson's name.

Laundry marks carefully erased by thieves are made visible again. So is the name tag on a coat on a body found after some months in the Thames. U.V. rays directed onto a heap of debris will cause fragments of bone or teeth to fluoresce, and save searchers hours of patient and unpleasant labor.

Now see how infra-red rays help the C.I.D. A man turns a dishonest penny by painting out the original address on a crate of goods in some railway goods yard, and substituting the name and address of his friend down a little back street who receives stolen property. The infra-red lamp will penetrate that paint, and reveal the original address.

In 1946, some boys playing in a bombed cellar stumbled upon a man's skeleton. There was no clue to his identity, and for all Scotland Yard knew, he might have been murdered.

The cellar floor was littered with hundreds of torn scraps of paper, all the writing on which was so coated with filth that no one could read it. Every scrap of that paper was examined under the infra-red lamp, which penetrated the dirt and grease, and on one scrap was found a name. That name was checked against the list of persons reported to Scotland Yard as missing, relatives were found, and it was established that the man had been an air-raid victim.

But even ultra-violet and infra-red do not complete the Photography Section's bag of tricks. You know, of course, that the marks on a bullet fired from any gun are as unique as fingerprints. During the war a man shot at the ticket collector on a London station. The bullet missed, and lodged in a wall, from which the C.I.D. took it. Two years passed. A suspected deserter was arrested, and when he was searched, a gun was found. It was thought from the man's record that this might be the gun used against the ticket collector two years before. So a photograph was taken showing the rifling marks on the station bullet. A test bullet was fired from the gun, and also photographed. Then the two photographs, greatly enlarged, were very carefully cut in half, and the left half of one joined to the right half of the other. They formed a perfect match, and the suspect had to answer for his old crime as well as for his later ones.

One final case from the Chief Inspector's collection. A man was walking across the road one night carrying a suitcase with a cloth cover. He was knocked down by a car which did not stop. Four days later a car was found which answered the description of the one involved in the accident. But there wasn't a mark on it and, of course, the driver had, so he said, been miles away when the accident happened. So the cameras went to work. A section of the car was photographed, and when the photographs were enlarged they showed clearly the impressions of a piece of cloth. The cloth cover of the suitcase was similarly photographed and enlarged. There was no doubt about the comparison— not, at least, to the jury who sent that driver to prison!

9

Criminals Under the Microscope

"IF MY EYES WOS A PAIR O' PATENT DOUBLE MILlion magnifyin' gas microscopes of hextra power," remarked the immortal Sam Weller in Charles Dickens's *Pickwick Papers*, "p'raps I might be able to see through a flight o' stairs and a deal door; but bein' only eyes, you see, my wision's limited."

The Scientific Laboratory at New Scotland Yard, having several patent double million "magnifyin' microscopes of hextra power," and a number of other useful gadgets besides, is not so limited in its "wision." It sees through much more than "a flight o' stairs and a deal door." It sees through criminals' stories, and that, to the C.I.D., is a vastly more important matter.

"There's nothing very interesting today, I'm afraid," said the police officer who took the writer of this book around the Laboratory. "There's an arsenic test going on; some woman tried to kill her husband by giving him arsenic in his bread-and-jam. They're working on a murder case in one of the labs. And there's a bit of a routine job here I've been working on myself."

The "routine" job was a slight case of shop-breaking. Someone had been rash enough to do it while snow lay on the ground, and had left foot-prints in the snow and had faintly heelmarked a piece of paper lying on the shop floor.

The local police had a very good idea who had done the job—they generally have—but they wanted convincing proof. They obtained a pair of the suspect's boots and sent them to the Laboratory, together with plaster casts of the footprints and the heelmark. The soles of the boots were photographed, and the footprints were photographed. Then the photographs were put side by side. Yes, there were those three lines forming a rough cross in exactly the same place on both photographs. There was the little circular spot where the rubber pattern had worn away. Just to make sure, transparent positives of the footprints were placed over positives of the boot soles. An exact fit. The same with the paper heelmark. Not a possible doubt that those Wellington boots had made the prints at the scene of the crime.

"Now these are one or two cases we've had at various times," said the police officer in the tones of a conjuror who is about to produce 19 white rabbits and five miles of colored flags from the top hat you know is perfectly empty. "Here's a piece of white handkerchief. Nothing to be seen, is there? Quite sure? Now look."

He pressed a switch, turned out the ordinary light, and the room was dimly lit by the soft glow of an ultra-violet lamp. He held the handkerchief under the lamp. The once-white handkerchief bore a clear, brownish circular stain in the middle of it. The story behind it ran as follows:

A man had started to rob a woman, pushing this handkerchief over her face. She shouted for help and people came running. She said that the man had tried to render her unconscious with chloroform or something else on this handkerchief. He denied it. As there was no sign of stain on the handkerchief, it was only her word against his.

So the handkerchief came up to the Laboratory and was put under the lamp. There were the characteristic brown rings left by ether, showing quite clearly.

The author of this book was shown an ordinary gummed address label still attached to part of the wrapping of a parcel which had been sent by rail. The name and address were quite clear on the label and the parcel had been delivered to the house of the addressee in the normal way. Nothing interesting here apparently nor anything to excite suspicion. But wait, let's see what happens when the rays from the ultra-violet lamp fall upon the label. There, clearly fluorescing, is another name and address quite different from the one we first saw. The story here was that the thief had erased the original name and address from the label by means of a chemical bleach which left no visible trace when viewed in ordinary light, and then substituted his own name and address and had the parcel delivered to him.

This remarkable lamp is in daily use in the Laboratory for detecting otherwise invisible stains on clothing; unseen laundry marks; differences in papers which otherwise appear identical; and in many other ways which give invaluable aid to investigating officers.

In another room there was a photomicrographic apparatus. Don't confuse photomicrography with microphotography. A microphotograph reduces a big thing to a small size, as when valuable historical documents are microphotographed for storage in a small space. A photomicrograph shows a small object very big.

A slide was put on the stage of the microscope and the focus was adjusted.

Through the microscope could be seen an enchanting pattern like a piece of lace.

"A section of plane tree," said the police officer. "We have a microtome, which is like a bacon slicer, only of course very much more delicate, which can take off a tiny section like that for examination. The one you're looking at now is cut horizontally and represents a cross-section of the tree. Now"—he pushed the slide along—"you're looking at a longitudinal section, that is, one cut lengthwise." He pushed the slide along again. "That's a radial section, cut down inside the tree, as it were. You'll see each pattern is different, but the pattern of each *kind* of wood is always the same."

The botanists of the Laboratory can identify most common woods as soon as they see them under the microscope. When they get a rare one, they may have to refer to their reference library in the biology laboratory, which holds hundreds of slides of different kinds of wood.

But the Laboratory scientists, like the police themselves, are only interested in arriving at the truth about a case. They will present only evidence of fact. Sometimes the facts they find clear someone who is suspected of a crime. The safe at a dog track was broken into one night. The C.I.D. men in charge of the case, helped by the Method Index, suspected two well-known safe-breakers, whose suits were obtained and sent to the Laboratory for examination, together with explosive residues from the safe and carpet fibers from the room where the safe was. The Laboratory could find no trace on the suits of the samples taken from the safe or the room. Therefore they said it was doubtful whether those men could have done that job.

There was another man accused of pig-stealing. Hairs taken from the front of his suit were sent to the Laboratory. It was found that they were rabbit's hairs, not a pig's, and the case against the suspect was dropped.

The Laboratory can identify any kind of hair or fiber—wood or other vegetable fibers; artificial fibers like nylon; human hair, animal hair, wool fibers. There was a case not long ago of housebreaking in Devon. Someone had seen a car behaving suspiciously, had taken the number and reported it. It was a London number, so the Devon police sent it up to the Yard with a request for inquiries to be made. The C.I.D. men traced the car, found it belonged to a firm who had hired it at that time to a certain man as a special favor. The hirer admitted having been in Devon, but denied any knowledge of the housebreaking.

Sweepings were taken from inside the car, and scientists carefully examined them. They did not know what had been stolen from the house, but among the sweepings they found hairs belonging to musquash, seal, dyed fox and undyed fox. They also found a number of brightly colored wool fibers which might have come from a carpet.

The Devon police were informed, and they revealed that among the goods stolen were a musquash fur coat, a baby seal coat, and blue fox and silver fox furs. But they couldn't identify the colored fibers—no carpet had been stolen. They were asked to have another look. They found that on the floor of the room from which the furs had been taken was a new Indian carpet. The thieves had picked up minute fibers from this on their shoes, transferred them to the floor of the car, and so gave the police further evidence helpful in securing their conviction.

The Laboratory performs this kind of near-miracle almost in its sleep, yet it is among the newest of the C.I.D.'s weapons in the war against crime. It was started in 1936, during the remarkable reign of Lord Trenchard at Scotland Yard. There were, of course, forensic scientists—"forensic" means anything to do with courts of law—who had helped Scotland Yard as private specialists. Sir Bernard Spilsbury, the famous pathologist, was one of them.

Although the Laboratory men will present only evidence of fact, sometimes they are asked their opinion, as expert witnesses. A man was tried for the murder of his parents-in-law at their Edgware home. He had at first denied any knowledge of the crime, but a C.I.D. officer who visited him at his own home very soon after the murders, heard the boiler roaring and, going to the kitchen, found the remains of a suit on the fire.

Little remained of the suit except the legs of the trousers, on which blood splashes were identified. The man then said that he *had* visited his parents-in-law, had found them dead on the floor, and had knelt beside them to see if they were dead. Then, becoming frightened, he had run away and tried to get rid of the suit.

When the Laboratory witness was giving his expert evidence in the case, he was asked whether the bloodstains on the trousers confirmed or denied this story. He gave it as his opinion that the stains were not in places where one might have expected to find them on the trousers of a kneeling man, but showed signs of having been splashed upwards.

A criminal will rarely be convicted on scientific evidence alone, however. The Laboratory's part is to clinch the police case, or sometimes, as we have seen, to disprove it.

Science is impartial, seeking only facts. The defence, in a case involving scientific evidence, is generally permitted to use the Scotland Yard Laboratory, to employ "outside" scientists to make their own tests, and given every facility for disproving the scientific evidence against the accused.

But you have not yet seen half the wonders of the Laboratory, as the next chapter will show.

10

The Clue of the Chip of Paint

"THIS IS THE BIOLOGY LAB," SAID THE POLICE officer, opening another door. He nodded casually at a bloodstained cloth on the bench. "That's a murder case they're working on," he said. "Just a routine blood test, I expect."

Blood tests are useful to the police in a variety of ways. There are at least three tests given to anything sent to the Laboratory as blood. The first is to touch it with a filter paper so that the paper takes a slight smear. The smear is then tested with a solution of benzedrine. If it turns a vivid blue or green color, it *may* be blood. If it doesn't change color, it definitely is not.

The second is the precipitin test. By using a prepared serum, the sample can be identified as human blood or as animal and, if the latter, as a particular kind of animal. Luckily for the Hampshire police, this test doesn't take very long.

They received a report that a lorry had knocked down a child in the road. The driver, it was said, had stopped, picked the injured child up, put her in the back of the lorry, and driven on. The police went to the spot, and there on the road was a stain of what looked like blood. They took a sample of it and sent it up to the Laboratory. Then they began hunting for the lorry, and for any little girls who might be missing.

Meanwhile, the Laboratory had tested the sample and found it was cow blood. This saved the police a great deal of time looking for a little girl who had never been knocked down because she had never existed. What *had* been knocked down was probably a calf, which someone from a distance might have mistaken for a child.

The third blood test is the grouping test. There are four main blood groups: O, A, B and AB. The commonest in white races are O and A. Between them they account for about 84 per cent. of the population. Twelve per cent. are B, and the remaining 4 per cent. are AB.

Sometimes the test works to clear a suspect. A woman had been murdered, and the C.I.D. suspected a particular man who had bloodstains on his clothing. His story was that he had had a fight with another man, whose nose had bled over his jacket. The Laboratory found that the bloodstains on the jacket didn't belong to the blood group of the murdered woman, and that was that.

In the Laboratory, beside a bench, there was a dummy figure which was used in testing the story of a farmer who had shot a man. His story was that he had gone out with his shotgun after poachers, and had stopped someone on his land. The man had gone at him with a stick, and in self-defence the farmer had fired two shots quite wildly from the hip. If his story was correct, well and good. But the police are suspicious people, and they must test everything, so they draped the clothes of the dead man over this dummy. It was seen at once that the shot-hole in the trousers was higher than the hole in the coat, which indicated that the dead man had had his arms stretched at the moment he was shot, as if he were delivering a blow. So the farmer's story was believed.

The physics section of the Laboratory provides some real wonders. You know that if you look through a prism when you hold it to the light it splits white light up into its visible components as well as the invisible ones. But in the physics laboratory there is a special prism. If you look at the ordinary daylight through it, then at the electric light, you would see different colors predominating. This prism is used in different ways.

The Hartridge Reversion Spectroscope, for instance, is an instrument for determining the amount of carbon monoxide in blood. Carbon monoxide is the deadly component of coal gas. When it enters the blood it forms a compound which absorbs certain bands in the spectrum.

A woman was found dead in her kitchen one day. Her head was in the gas oven, and the gas was on. It would have been thought an ordinary case of suicide, except that the doctor who went to the house didn't quite like the way her body was lying. He sent a sample of her blood to the Laboratory, and there it was carefully examined by means of the special spectroscope. The spectroscope revealed that the woman hadn't been gassed, and it was afterwards found that she had been strangled by her husband, and put in the gas oven afterwards.

That is comparatively simple. Spectrography is rather more complicated. The Laboratory received from the police a chip of paint about the size of a thumbnail. It had been picked up on the road where a cyclist had been run over and killed by a motorist who hadn't stopped. The police thought the paint might have come from the car. Could the Laboratory give them any help with it?

The Laboratory was able to tell them that the car had originally been painted black, that it had been repainted once in rather a hurry, had been painted three times again since, and was now black once more.

The local police thought about this information from the Laboratory, and someone remembered a local motorist who was always bumping into things with his car and having to have the fenders repainted. The police went to see him. They found a dent in the car just about where a cyclist's head might have struck. They found a flake chipped out of the fender which matched the flake found on the road. That still wasn't enough. They took a chip of paint from the car fender, and sent it to the Laboratory. There it was examined, and the Laboratory was able to say that the paint from the fender was identical with the paint found in the road. It was also found that on the fender were almost invisible flakings of paint similar to those from the cycle which had been hit. And that was enough.

All this testing was done by a combination of spectroscopy and photography which is called spectrography. Anything that emits light can be analyzed. A tiny sample of the thing to be analyzed—in this case a minute part of the flake of paint—is placed on the spectrograph's electrodes. The electrodes vaporize it, and the light which is emitted is broken up by an arrangement of prisms and photographed against a wave-length scale. Each element (and there are 94 known elements, such as carbon, oxygen, hydrogen and so on) will emit its own characteristic spectrum which appears in exactly the same place against that scale in the photograph. One lot of paint, analyzed like that, is not exactly the same as any other lot of paint. The paint from the top of a tin isn't even exactly like the paint from the bottom of the same tin. So the Laboratory was able to analyze the 17 coats which formed that single small flake of paint, and to say from the irregularities that on one occasion the car might have been painted in a hurry without allowing the undercoat time to dry. Of course when the other samples were received, they were spectrographed too, and compared with the original clue.

That's one example of the spectrograph's use.

There are plenty of others. If someone's suspected of safe-breaking, the Laboratory can check particles of metal from the safe against particles found on the suspect's clothing.

As we have seen before, it is impossible to commit any kind of crime without leaving *some* kind of clue. Whether the clue can lead to conviction is another matter, despite the skill of the Laboratory. There was a clever fellow once who was suspected of stealing from a safe in a cinema. He had hidden in the building until everyone had left for the night, done the job, and broken out of the cinema. The Laboratory tested his clothing, and found nothing to connect him with the crime. It turned out afterwards that he'd been to prison before as a result of the Laboratory's work, and had made up his mind to beat them. So he stripped off all his clothing, and worked naked! But the police got him in some other way.

Remarkable though the work of the Laboratory is, only two police cases in every hundred call for Laboratory help. The other 98 cases are cleared up by hard routine work on the beat or in the divisional C.I.D. And even in the two cases which go to the Laboratory, the man on the spot has to know what kind of clue the Laboratory can help him with, he has to hunt until he finds it, and he has to put the Laboratory's help to the best use, as the local constable did when he traced the driver who was always having bumps with his car.

11

Criminal Investigation Department

A DETECTIVE-SERGEANT OF THE CRIMINAL INVES-
tigation Department worked on a case from July
until November. He interviewed many dozens of
people. He took between 40 and 50 statements. He
collected 115 exhibits. He brought the case to court
and secured a conviction.

The same detective-sergeant helped his divisional
Chief Inspector in another case. It took many weeks,
many dozens of people were interviewed, many
statements were taken and exhibits collected. This
case also was taken to court, and a conviction
secured.

The first case made no newspaper headlines. The
criminal had stolen building scaffolding worth several thousand pounds, but that is not news.

The second case was world-famous. It was that of
the murderer Neville Heath, and everyone was very
happy when he was out of the way.

But the detective-sergeant thinks he did more
hard, solid work on the first case, about which few
people have ever heard.

In smaller police forces, when a uniformed police
constable gets on the trail of a crime, he quite
possibly changes into plain clothes, does his own

detective work, catches his crook, and takes his case into court. In such a large area as London, this system would be impossible, for inquiries may take days, weeks, months, and during that time a man with highly specialized knowledge would be taken away from his proper job of patrolling the beat, or the river, or in one of the radio cars. Unless in exceptional circumstances, therefore, such as that of the observer of radio car 5D in our first chapter, who caught his man red-handed, the uniformed officer hands over the detection of crime which has already been committed to another body of specially selected and trained men, the C.I.D. The uniformed branch, you might say, is responsible for the prevention of crime; the plain clothes branch, the C.I.D., is responsible for its detection.

Some members of the uniformed branch grumble about this. There are caustic references to the "glamor boys" of the C.I.D., who get most of the glory while the uniformed branch does the work. But when you ask a uniformed man what else could be done, he agrees that it is the only system which would work.

Besides, most of the C.I.D.'s work is unspectacular, like that of the detective-sergeant making his long, painstaking inquiries into the theft of building scaffolding. A typical division's monthly "crime chart" looks something like this:

   1 burglary
  22 cases of housebreaking

40 cases of shopbreaking

4 breaking attempts

1 case of possessing housebreaking tools

3 cases of robbery and assault

2 cases of larceny from the person

73 cases of larceny from a house

17 cases of stealing motor-cars

38 cases of stealing bicycles

37 cases of stealing from vehicles

7 cases of stealing from telephone boxes

4 cases of receiving

All this means much hard work for the C.I.D., and not a great deal of glory. There were 20 cases of murder in London in 1950, all except one cleared up by the year's end; but 5,000 people were killed or seriously injured in traffic accidents. Long weeks go by, and the C.I.D.'s "Murder Bags," which you read about in Chapter Seven, accumulate dust on their shelves. But the C.I.D. is working away quietly at its housebreakings and larcenies and thefts of motorcars, day in, day out, with long hours, irregular meals, and sometimes 48 hours on the trot without sleep.

There are 1,464 men and women in the C.I.D., including the Assistant Commissioner, and most of these work outside Scotland Yard.

Under the Assistant Commissioner are a Commander and a Deputy Commander. All of these except the Assistant Commissioner, who is a lawyer, have worked their way up from the beat.

The Chief Inspector of the Metropolitan Police Detective Training School sums up the qualities which make a good detective. "Zeal, tact, good address, personality, persistence, and the ability to merge oneself with one's surroundings, like a chameleon. The detective must be able to talk to peers and dustmen on equal terms. And he mustn't, whatever the circumstances, be a clock-watcher. When you've got an important case on your plate, everything else has to go—meals, sleep, wife, home—until you're satisfied that all immediate matters have been dealt with."

We left our probationer constable in Chapter Four, you'll remember, deciding that he wants to join the C.I.D. If he has all the qualities noted above—and, what is more important, has had them brought to the notice of his divisional C.I.D. inspector—he will be attached to the C.I.D. as an "aid." This trial run may last 12 months, more or less. If the average aid shows normal skill at his work, he goes before a Selection Board, and if successful becomes a probationer detective constable, hands in his uniform, and works with the C.I.D. for a year. During that time he will probably be given a 10-weeks' intensive course at the Detective Training School. If he passes the final examination there—it is stiff, and many fail—he will be permanently appointed to the C.I.D.

Here is an observation test used at the School, which you can try for yourself. An unexpected visitor will come into the room where the class is sitting. No comment will be made about him to the class, but perhaps half an hour after he has gone, students will be asked to describe him. They must not only say whether he is dark or fair or wears glasses or a brown suit, but really *describe* him so that, should need arise, his description could be circulated all over the country, with a fair chance that some constable patrolling his beat can recognize the man from that description alone.

Here are the points the students are expected to cover in their answers: the man's approximate age; his height and build; the color of his hair, eyebrows and eyes; what kind of forehead he has; his nose, mouth, lips and chin; his teeth; his ears and face; his complexion; any outstanding marks or peculiarities of manner; his dress.

There is a variation on this. The students form two lines, and between them two strangers will walk at an ordinary pace. Then the students must return to their classroom and write down a description of one of the men but as if he were dressed in the clothes of the other. The importance of this you can see for yourself. A criminal on the run will change his clothes if he can; and a man may not look quite the same in a brown suit as in a blue one. Try it yourself with some of your friends. It is trickier than it sounds.

There are many other things the students must learn. They must know the law, of course, inside

out and upside down and backwards and forwards.
They must know when they have power to arrest
a man with and without a warrant. They must know
how to search someone very thoroughly. There is
an exhibit in the School's museum, an ordinary box
of safety matches. It was found in a man's pocket.
A careless searcher would have looked at it, shaken
it perhaps, and laid it aside. But the detective who
found it opened it as well. He saw nothing unusual—
just a box full of matches. He went a step further,
emptied out the matches. The box was only half
full of matches. But under the top layers it was
half full of dope, which is what the detective was
looking for.

The students must know how to search not only
a man, but a vehicle also. Dummy petrol-tanks full
of smuggled watches, smuggled nylons packed away
inside the cover of a spare tire—nothing can be taken
on trust.

They must know a little about thieves' slang, for
it serves as a code in which crooks may discuss their
dark doings without the outsider understanding. "I
had nearly drawn that old flat's skin, but he balked
me," John Townsend of the Bow Street runners
heard a man say in the street one day. He arrested
the man on the spot, for "to draw a skin" meant to
steal a purse. Thieves' slang is always changing—it
would no longer be a safe code if it didn't—so the
detective must keep constantly up to date.

But above all the detective must know the near-miracle workers of his own department in New Scotland Yard, for although 99 per cent. of the C.I.D.'s work is blood, sweat, toil and tears, that other 1 per cent.—which is usually *the* big case—couldn't be solved without the Finger Print Branch, or C.R.O., or the Laboratory, or the Flying Squad. Some of them you have already met; others you will meet in later chapters, but here is a summary of what each department does.

There are eight branches of the Criminal Investigation Department, plus the Special Branch and the Scientific Laboratory.

C1 is the Central Office, which deals with crimes of special importance, such as murders. When the detective from Scotland Yard is called in by some provincial force, that detective comes from C1; and C1 also deals with cases requiring investigation abroad, or co-operation with foreign forces.

Not many years ago Scotland Yard "received information"—you will always come back to some variations on that phrase!—about a plot to flood the country with forged insurance stamps, which being printed in Warsaw. A Chief Inspector was given the case, and after tedious work he induced a Pole living in London to go to Warsaw and make contact with the forgers. The Pole was able to persuade these men to come to London, saying that he had a ready market for the stamps, and three members of the gang left Warsaw for London. Scotland Yard, of course, had knowledge of all their movements, and when they arrived at Harwich they were followed by detectives.

The police waited until they had reached their hotel and sorted out their baggage containing the forged stamps. Then Scotland Yard stepped in and scooped the pool. The Chief Inspector left the same night by air for Warsaw, with the information secured from the men arrested in London. Helped by the Polish police, he traced the forgers' three dens, raided them, and found that they were also forging Polish bonds and American dollar notes. As a result of his work 15 people were arrested in Warsaw, besides the three in London.

C2 department of the C.I.D. deals with all papers relating to crime and suspected crime except those which concern C3 and 4 and the Special Branch. It sees to the deportation of undesirable aliens, and keeps an eye on national registration offences.

C3 is the Finger Print Branch. Fingerprints receive so much publicity in the press and in detective novels that for years C3 has been living in dread that crooks would become careful enough to leave no fingerprints behind them. But they nearly always do. One criminal was especially careful to carry a soft brush around with him, and to brush everything he had touched before he left the scene of his robberies. He forgot only one print—that on the outside window ledge as he climbed down. He had plenty of time in prison afterwards to consider his forgetfulness.

C4 is the Criminal Record Office. It contains the record and photograph of everyone who has ever been convicted of a criminal offence anywhere in the British Isles and in many foreign countries also; compiles the *Police Gazette* and its supplements; keeps an eye on prisoners on parole; and runs the amazing index of methods criminals use to carry out their jobs, described in Chapter Six.

C5 is the "housekeeping" branch, dealing with promotions, commendations, discipline and orders.

C6 is the Fraud Squad, in which the Metropolitan Police co-operate with the City of London police to prevent and detect shady company deals, issues of bogus shares and prospectuses, and the like.

C7 is the Detective Training School.

C8 is the famous Flying Squad.

Then there is the Special Branch, which guards visiting Royalty, important visitors and politicians. The Metropolitan Police have special powers of arrest within 10 miles of any Royal residence, so that they can cope with any crime against Royalty within 10 miles of Windsor Castle or Sandringham or Balmoral.

Last of all is the Scientific Laboratory, where they will tell you what kind of tree a grain of sawdust comes from, how many coats of paint a car has had, and other wonderful things.

But all these branches can only work as well as the divisional C.I.D. men on the job will let them. A careless movement—and there is a fingerprint blurred forever. And that grain of sawdust has to be found and sent to the Laboratory before the scientists can do anything about it. So in the last resort everything comes back to the detective constable or the uniformed policeman going about his daily routine. If he is good, Scotland Yard is good. If he is bad, not even the most elaborate camera or microscope can do anything about it.

Here is a fairly typical divisional C.I.D. case, perhaps a little more exciting than most, which shows several of the branches helping the man on the spot.

About 8 o'clock one Sunday morning, three men were seen loading parcels onto a car outside a big store. They drove off, and 10 minutes later the car was found empty and abandoned. Three hundred pounds' worth of goods had been taken from the store, and the three men had changed their clothes there, leaving their old ones behind. They had also left fingerprints. From these prints one man was identified by the Finger Print Branch. C.R.O. had his description, photograph and record, showing that he was wanted already for armed robbery and for escaping from police custody.

Three weeks passed, during which the divisional C.I.D. interviewed dozens of people and made dozens of routine inquiries. One evening they received a phone call—"information received" again!—to say that this man was going to call briefly at a public house on the other side of London in a very short while. The men on the spot couldn't possibly have got across London by the time stated, so the local C.I.D. were asked to pick up the man, whose description had been circulated to all stations by C.R.O.

The local men arrived at the public house and waited. No sign of the suspect. They thought they must have arrived too late, or that the information given had been false. It often is false, sometimes deliberately false to attract the C.I.D.'s attention from one spot where something is going to happen to another spot where nothing is going to happen.

In due course the detectives left the public house. Next door was a café, and as they passed one of them chanced to look through the café window. There sat the suspect, innocent as a lamb, over a cup of tea.

The other two men were picked up in due course, in another stolen car, wearing clothes taken from the store.

Now take this case to pieces. Finger Prints and C.R.O. play their part. So does the ordinary civilian-in-the-street who first reported a suspicious happening on a Sunday morning, and Information Room which put out the radio message which sent a patrol car straightaway to find the thieves' abandoned vehicle. There is also the courage of the detectives who made the arrest, for men wanted for armed robbery do not always surrender without a struggle. There is a lot of luck. But at the bottom there are those three weeks of slogging hard work by divisional plain-clothes men.

And now for a closer look at the men of the Central Office.

12

The Man From the Yard

THE CENTRAL OFFICE OF THE CRIMINAL INVESTI-gation Department consists of a chief superintendent, seven superintendents, 14 chief inspectors, 4 detective inspectors, 18 first-class and 18 second-class detective sergeants, and 26 detective constables. There are also a chief inspector, a sergeant and two detective constables of the women police, engaged in crimes concerning women and young children.

All these men and women are especially selected because of their skill in detection, for to Central Office come many of the most famous cases not only of the Metropolitan Police area, but from the provinces and from abroad as well. "The Man from Scotland Yard" called in by a provincial force to solve some crime comes from Central Office, and to Central Office go difficult or unusual cases from many parts of the world.

If it is thought that the new Parliament building is being sabotaged by a modern Guy Fawkes, Central

Office is called in to investigate. If civilian planes are
being sold and flown to the Middle East, Central
Office combines with foreign forces to discover the details. If Europe is being flooded with Bank of England notes forged by the German Government during
the Second World War, Central Office detectives
will be found working with their German, French,
Dutch, Belgian colleagues to clear up the chaos.

Here is an exciting forgery case followed over
several years by a chief inspector of Central Office
which shows Scotland Yard's long reach and wide
memory at their best.

It began in 1934, when the chief inspector was
in Berlin inquiring into the spread of forged £10
and £5 Bank of England notes. To carry out his
inquiries, he posed as an Englishman living in Ant-
werp who wanted to buy forged English notes. So
that he could show the suspected forgers he had
plenty of money with which to buy the notes, the
German police had supplied him with a thick wad
of forged German notes. He flourished these whenever paying bills, keeping on top of the forgeries a
few genuine German notes. The German police had
told him that they were being plagued by these
forged German notes, but had no idea who was
forging them, or where they were coming from.

The chief inspector cleared up his English forgery
case, and returned to England. Nearly two years
passed. A new type of forged £5 and £10 bank
note began to be received by the Bank of England

from various banks. Their source was found to be
Paris, and the chief inspector was detailed to take
up this new case. He visited Paris, got in touch with
the French police, but found they had no information about the forgeries. So he set about the hard
routine task of inquiry. He visited all the banks,
money exchange offices, large hotels and other places
in Paris where English bank notes of £5 and upward
were likely to be tendered. He saw all the managers,
pointed out to them how they could distinguish the
forgeries, and asked them to detain on some pre-
text anyone who presented a forged note and to send
for the police. Satisfied that he had done all that
could be done in Paris, he returned to London.

A few weeks later, a man went into a money exchange office in Paris, and presented several £10
and £5 notes. On examination the cashier found
these to be forgeries. He called the police, the man
was taken into custody and found to have 23 forged
£10 notes and 27 forged £5 notes on him. But he
refused to give any particulars about himself, except
to say that the notes had been given him by a person in a Luxemburg café.

The chief inspector went over from London and
questioned him. At the time of the interview, the
suspect was feigning madness, and no sense could
be got out of him. But the chief inspector noticed
that although he spoke English with a broken accent,
he used idiomatic phrases which seemed to indicate
that he had lived in England. The chief inspector

then had him stripped, but found that almost every label or other identifying mark had been removed from his clothes. There was, however, just one mark on his shirt—a laundry mark which the inspector decided was English.

He returned to London, and arranged for every laundry to be visited by the police, and the address taken of every person having that laundry mark. There were some scores of these, and it took nine days to work through them. But one of the addresses, in northwest London, turned out to be an empty house which had been occupied for some years by a German known as a photographer. The chief inspector learned that this man had lived there with his niece, had gone abroad towards the end of June—the month in which the forged notes began to appear in Paris—and had not returned. Some two weeks after he had gone, the neighbors said, a lot of smoke was seen coming from the chimneys of the house. The niece had disappeared. There was a considerable amount of rent owing, and the house agents had sold the contents of the house, and advertised it for letting again.

The chief inspector then inquired whether the niece had had any men friends. This trail led him to a man working in a garage, from whom he learned that the niece had suddenly gone to Brussels. The man had her address, which he gave to the chief inspector.

At the same time, a man who had worked for the photographer said that the German used to lock himself up in a basement room for three or four days at a time. After that he would go for a continental trip, to Belgium or Germany, and return with plenty of money.

The chief inspector went to the basement room. It was empty, but he had no doubt that he stood in the forger's den. At the end of a day's work, he thought, the floor would be littered with paper and other odds and ends, which the German would sweep up and burn in the stove. But there was just a chance that some incriminating fragment might have gone down between the floorboards. He decided to take up a board at the edge of the fireplace, and see what he could find. He groped in the dirt underneath—and pulled up the negative of a German 50-mark note, which he immediately recognized as the negative of the notes he had handled in Berlin in 1934. He took up more boards, and found several partly broken and melted metal plates bearing the watermarks of Bank of England and Belgian notes.

That same day he left by air for Brussels. He told the Belgian police what he had found, and with a Belgian inspector went to the address which had been given him by the niece's acquaintance. At the very moment of their arrival, she was coming out with her packed luggage. Her young man in England had telegraphed to say that police inquiries were being made, and she was in the very act of getting away.

She was taken to police headquarters and questioned. She said that she knew nothing about the
forgeries, but that in June her uncle had left for
Paris, saying he would be away only a few days.
He had not returned, she had had no news of him,
and, looking around in the cupboards of the basement room, she found negatives, partly printed bank
notes and metal plates bearing watermarks. She immediately realized what her uncle was up to, and
tried to burn the incriminating evidence. That was
the cloud of smoke which neighbors had seen. The
metal plates, which would not burn entirely away,
she had stuffed under the floorboards.

With this evidence, the chief inspector and his
Belgian colleague hastened to Paris, where the man
who had presented the forged English notes was still
being detained. When he learned that his niece had
been arrested in Brussels, he abandoned all pretence
of being insane. He made a full confession and, after
being brought back to England, was sentenced to
four years' penal servitude for forgery.

An important part of Central Office's duty lies
in co-operation with provincial British forces. The
decision whether or not Scotland Yard should be
called in rests always with the Chief Constable of
the town or county in which the crime has been
committed. When the Yard *is* called in, the local
force always co-operates warmly and wholeheartedly
with the man from London. Central Office men are
not necessarily better detectives than provincial

C.I.D. officers, but it is recognized that they may have had considerably wider experience with serious cases.

Let us see what happens when a superintendent or chief inspector of Scotland Yard is called in to help the local police investigate a murder or other serious crime.

At 5 o'clock one evening an old lady is found murdered in a West Country pub, her money stolen. Local police investigate, and find little to help them. Late that night, the Chief Constable telephones the chief inspector on duty at Central Office, and asks for help. The chief inspector telephones the home of some sleeping senior officer of Central Office, and hands over the case to him. The officer selects a Central Office sergeant who is free of other duties and who works well with him. They pack, get the fullest possible details from Scotland Yard, and are off by car to the scene of the crime.

When they arrive, they find that heavy rain has washed out all helpful footprints, that the local C.I.D. have already investigated the possibility of fingerprints and drawn a blank. But a towel on the counter of the pub seems to indicate one thing— that the murderer is a man who may have been in trouble before, and knows enough about finger-prints to have wiped away traces.

The Central Office man's first action is to seal off the area as far as possible, and to examine every-one within it who may have useful information.

Small, but possibly vital, details are learned. In this quiet country place, for instance, there is a long-standing feud between two sections of the population. The landlady, old though she was, had thrown out troublemakers from her pub. She was a strong old lady, and the man who killed her must have been fairly strong too. Was there someone engaged in that feud whom she had thrown out and who bore a grudge against her?

All the local men are checked. At the time of the crime, they were away together at a football match. Nothing doing there.

What about people discharged from the nearest jail? Another check, another blank. Any local suspected characters? More checking, more blanks. Then two or three girls are found in a nearby office, and they remember something. They had seen a man near the pub some time before the murder, and they can give his description. A call goes out to trace the man. Time passes, and he is found and questioned. He is a commercial traveler, a stranger to the place, who was waiting for some passer-by of whom he could ask the way. As the murderer had, obviously, known the pub very well, the commercial traveler was eliminated as a suspect, especially as he proved that he was elsewhere at the time of the murder.

More time spent, but not wasted—for everything, literally *everything*, has to be investigated. It *may* lead to a dead end, as in the case of the commercial traveler. But the detective never knows where anything will lead. Out of dozens of inquiries, dozens of statements, there may be perhaps 15 or 20 incidents like that of the commercial traveler, each of which must be followed up.

The man from the Yard is on his own. He asks the local force for what help he wants in taking statements or following clues, but he and he alone is in charge of the investigation. There is no interference from Scotland Yard. He reports back to the local Chief Constable and, of course, he has all the wonderful resources of the Yard behind him. If the days pass without result and he feels that he is getting nowhere, he may go back to London for a conference with other Central Office men. All the statements and investigations will be reviewed by fresh brains, and they may be able to throw helpful light on the matter. But it is still the one man's case. He stands or falls on his own decision.

Chatting to local people—chatting, but never casually, always with the one end in view—the superintendent in charge of this case happened upon a tiny incident. Shortly after the murder and robbery, a local man had been visited by another man who owed him some money. This second man had worked in the neighborhood, but had given up his job a little time before, and now lived 40 miles away. He had paid his debt, rather unexpectedly, and had paid it mostly in half-crowns and florins. The murdered old lady had had a large collection of half-crowns and florins. Small coins she used for change in the bar, but her half-crowns and florins she had kept.

It was such a little thing, only one of many such incidents reported and investigated. But the other lines of inquiry petered out one by one, and this did not. The man living 40 miles away had been spending money very freely since the murder. He knew the pub, and the old lady's habits. A lot of the money he was spending was in half-crowns and florins. Little by little the superintendent traced the suspect's movements through the days before the murder, through the fateful day itself, until he had tracked his man to within a half a mile of the scene of the crime. Then there was a blank. No one had seen him, no one knew anything.

The superintendent and his sergeant interviewed the suspect, who, of course, denied all knowledge of the crime. But there were half-crowns and florins in his possession. These were sent to the Home Office Laboratory, and on some of them were found specks of blood so minute that it was only just possible to identify them as human blood. But it might be the suspect's own blood; he might have cut himself. A careful search was made to see if he had. There was not a cut or a scratch on him.

Meanwhile, the sergeant had found something else. There had been a fire in the man's grate, and the sergeant had taken out a charred mass of paper and other things, which had been sent to the Laboratory for analysis. In the mass were some hard black objects which could not be identified. Then someone suggested that they should be shown to a jewelry expert. The jewelry expert saw them, and identified them as the charred remains of a string of old-fashioned artificial pearls. The old lady had had such a string. And the suspect could not say how these pearls had got into his grate.

Little by little the net closed. The man was arrested, charged, and tried. He strenuously contested the evidence against him, but the jury found it sufficient, and their verdict was "Guilty."

You will notice both in this case and the forgery case that detection is a matter of patience, routine work, more patience—and luck. This same superintendent of Central Office was on a wartime case in which luck was the only thing on his side.

At five o'clock one morning, in the blackout of wartime London, a soldier in a helmet which hid his face, tried to hold up the barman of a pub, and shot him dead. The soldier escaped into the blackout, and vanished. He had touched nothing in the pub; there wasn't a clue against him. And in wartime Britain there were some millions of soldiers of all nationalities.

But this soldier was a Canadian and he telephoned to a friend in the Military Police to say that he was in desperate trouble, and what should he do. The friend in the Military Police was also a friend of the superintendent at Central Office. *He* telephoned the superintendent to ask what advice he should give *his* friend. The superintendent knew about the murder in the pub. He put two and two together—and the man was caught.

13

Tracking the Fraudsman

In c.r.o.'s method index of crimes, about half the space is taken up by fraud. People who pose as actors, advertising agents or dentists; people who run bogus charitable societies or registry offices; people who specialize in defrauding clergymen or women or tradesmen: they are all there, and a very nasty crowd they are.

But there are some frauds, company frauds, on such a gigantic scale that in 1946 a special branch of the C.I.D. was formed to deal with them.

The Fraud Squad was set up after the Second World War because it was thought that in the backwash of war there would be many large and small investment frauds, as there had been after the First World War. Ex-servicemen came home with their small bonuses, looked for a livelihood and an investment. There would be an attractive advertisement in some newspaper, saying that if the ex-serviceman liked to invest his bonus in the advertiser's business, he would be assured of a good job, a fixed income and a directorship.

Many ex-servicemen fell for it. Within a few weeks their bonuses had vanished, and the companies had vanished too. Well, this did happen again to some extent after the Second World War, but the Fraud Squad stopped it in double-quick time. They nosed out the false advertisers, brought two or three quick prosecutions before any ex-serviceman had parted with his money, and secured convictions which made fraudsmen think twice about that particular way of earning a living.

If the Fraud Squad had done nothing more than that, it would have earned the undying gratitude of thousands of ex-servicemen. But there was bigger game, as the following case illustrates.

A very respected citizen of the world had been paying over money to a woman who said that she was investing it for him in the leaseholds of houses. Everything seemed to be aboveboard. The man was telephoned by estate agents and solicitors, who seemed to be perfectly reputable people engaged in a perfectly reputable deal.

At various times, the man gave the woman a total of £36,000 to invest. But always something happened which made her want more money. One day she came to him with the story that she had sent a large sum of money by hand to pay taxes on some houses, and the money had been stolen. Could she have more money for the taxes?

The man was still unsuspicious, but he thought the theft of such a large sum of money must be reported to the police. It was reported, and the police found that there had been no such theft. The Fraud Squad followed the case up from there, and found that all the "solicitors," "estate agents" and the rest had been the woman's confederates. Not a single house had been bought with that £36,000. The whole story from beginning to end was one gigantic fraud.

Another of the Fraud Squad's big cases took them ranging over a great part of West Africa. An enterprising gentleman in London formed a company calling itself by a fine, high-sounding name. The offices of this splendid-sounding company consisted of one small and rather shabby bedroom. But the unfortunate West Africans did not know that. They read advertisements in their local papers proclaiming that the company with the fine, high-sounding name required agents in Africa. These should be prepared to put down deposits of money as guarantees of their substance and good faith. In return for these deposits the splendid-sounding West African company promised to make them sole local agents for whatever they chose to sell, from motorcars to bicycle pumps.

Of course, it cost more to become an agent for motorcars than for bicycle pumps, and some unfortunates in West Africa parted with as much as £2,000, and received no motorcars in return.

The Fraud Squad located the swindler in London, and investigated the case in Nigeria and other

West African territories. Then it brought witnesses to London, and got the fraudsman sentenced to 5 years' imprisonment.

Members of the Fraud Squad have every opportunity to become widely traveled men, for cases have taken their detectives all over Europe and far beyond. But the Fraud Squad man needs exceptional qualifications. He must take a course in company law and accountancy, must be of good appearance, must have more than average education and intelligence, and must be prepared to set himself to master what is for many a new and tricky corner of the law.

Since the Fraud Squad was formed, police officers from Liverpool, Manchester, Cardiff, Bristol, Birmingham and other big cities have come to Scotland Yard for training in its method of work. As a result, it is becoming increasingly difficult for the sharepusher, the promoter of fraudulent companies, to make his dishonest living.

14

The Flying Squad

THE FLYING SQUAD SERGEANT WAS GIVING EVIdence in court.

"I followed the accused in a motor vehicle," he said.

"What kind of a motor vehicle, sergeant?" asked the magistrate.

"Just a motor vehicle, Your Worship," said the sergeant respectfully but very firmly; and no more would he say, for the Flying Squad prefers to move in a mysterious way to carry out its duties.

The Flying Squad was formed after the First World War, with the idea of having a mobile body of detectives for special duty, to deal with particular outbreaks of crime, or for operations in any part of the Metropolitan Police area. It was so successful that it was soon enlarged and extended, and newspapers began to credit the Flying Squad with captures so amazing that it struck terror into the hearts of criminals. Some of these captures were not made by the Flying Squad at all, but by ordinary police cars. Nevertheless, the Flying Squad does work wonders, and its chief is always among Scotland Yard's best-known personalities.

Here is an example of the skill and intelligence which brought its present head to his high position.

At about midday one day some years ago, a rent collector was found unconscious on the ground floor of a Paddington tenement. He was taken to a hospital, but was quite unable to say how he had been injured. It looked as if he must have fallen downstairs, striking his head as he fell.

The sergeant of the C.I.D., who is now Chief Superintendent of the Flying Squad, had meanwhile been examining the place where the rent collector had been found. He noticed that while many of the man's belongings were strewn about, the satchel containing the cash he had collected was missing. So the sergeant began the usual routine questioning of everyone in the house. He worked his way from the top floor down to the basement, and in the basement he found a man who seemed very hesitant in his answers and was obviously uneasy.

The man said he was out of work, but the sergeant noticed that his breath smelled of whisky— a luxury, even in those days, for unemployed men. The man admitted that he *had* been drinking, had been in a public house from about noon until about half-past twelve. Moreover, at about twenty past twelve, he had taken a whisky which tasted funny, and had spat it out over the counter. He suggested that the sergeant ask the barman about it, for he would be sure to remember the incident, and of course that would be an alibi.

Of course. The sergeant thought it sounded too much like the kind of thing a man would do who wanted to attract attention to himself for the purpose of an alibi. But it would be an alibi difficult to shake, for the pub was a busy pub, and the barman would almost certainly have difficulty in swearing to the exact time.

But now the sergeant noticed something else. When he bent down to look under the bed for any weapon with which the crime might have been committed, he noticed that the man was wearing no socks. No, said the man, it was a hot day and he had taken them off. The sergeant remembered having found a sock near where the injured man had lain, together with a little heap of dirt. A sock filled with such dirt, he thought, would make a pretty useful weapon. He decided the man must be detained for further questioning.

Then he went to the public house where the man said he had been. Here he had a stroke of well-deserved luck. Normally, the barman wouldn't have remembered the time of the spitting incident, but that day, as it happened, he had asked the boss's permission to leave just before midday, to meet a relative at Paddington Station. He had been keeping his eye on the clock, and the spitting had occurred, not at twenty minutes past twelve, but at about three minutes to twelve. Moreover, the whisky-spitter had left the pub *before* the barman; that is to say, before midday. Bang went the alibi!

The Flying Squad work in plain clothes, using motorcars of many types which bear no outward sign of their police ownership, and which were among the first police vehicles to be equipped with wireless.

The members of the Squad also keep their ears well to the ground, know many habitual criminals and their haunts from personal experience. A telephone will ring in a Flying Squad man's flat: "That you, Guv? Lofty Joe's doin' a job down the Old

Kent Road tonight." Away will speed a Flying Squad vehicle, indistinguishable from any civilian car, and Lofty Joe, when he arrives, will be given a warm welcome.

In this way, working very much under cover and acting on "information received" so secret that often no one outside a handful of Flying Squad officers knows where it comes from, the Squad keeps long and patient observation on criminals and their crimes.

For some time before 1948, for instance, the authorities had been gravely perturbed at the circulation in London of large numbers of forged clothing coupons. As clothing was being strictly rationed, the circulation of these bogus coupons presented a serious problem.

A detective inspector of the Flying Squad was selected to pick the officers he wanted to work with him, and to trace the coupons to their source.

He investigated a woman who said that she was a dressmaker, living in the Notting Hill district. The inspector and his officers, both men and women, followed this woman for many weeks, seeing her get rid of forged coupons. But she was not the person they wanted. They were after the forger himself.

They trailed the woman to all parts of London, and they noticed that several of her visits to the East End and the Docks coincided with considerable thefts of cloth and other rationed material from riverside premises. The C.I.D. men of the Thames Division were put to work to take care of *that*, and the inspector went on watching.

The trail led at last to an address in Maida Vale. The premises were watched, and the inspector decided on a raid.

The police went in and found, actually working on the press, a man named William Roberts who had a long criminal record. The apparatus he was using, the plates for printing clothing coupons, made by himself, were of the highest quality.

Simultaneously with the raid on Roberts, the inspector organized raids on other addresses to which his officers had traced persons known to have been disposing of the forged coupons. As the result of the night's work—a night's work, but following on many weeks of careful watching and shadowing— there was an end to that particular outbreak of forgery.

Perhaps the most wonderful of the Squad's recent cases, however, is a story of cold-blooded heroism which makes adventure novels look silly.

Early in 1947 "information was received" that a gang of thieves proposed to waylay an official of the Kentish Town Branch of the Midland Bank, steal his keys, and then rob the bank. It was learned that for some time members of the gang had been watching and following the bank official, to become familiar with his habits and movements when he left the bank to return home. It was also learned that the place where he would be waylaid had been decided upon and a plan made for his disposal after the bank had been robbed.

This information led the C.I.D. to believe that the gang would be split up. One part of it would waylay the official while other members waited near the bank. The C.I.D. wanted to scoop in the whole gang; but to do this it was necessary to let the attack take place, and leave the attackers free to join their mates near the bank.

The bank authorities were consulted, and they agreed to allow a police officer to impersonate the bank official and let himself be waylaid and beaten up.

Detective Sergeant Deans of the Flying Squad, who was similar in build and appearance to the bank official, volunteered for this dangerous duty. He knew what the assignment meant—and he took it on in cold blood.

On the evening of February 21st, Deans, wearing some of the bank official's clothes, locked the bank doors and set off to the bank official's home. As he entered Kentish Town Railway Station he noticed that two men who had followed him on a previous occasion were on the platform. When he left the train at Woodside Park, the two men also got out.

Deans walked calmly down the footpath from the station and saw that the two men had been joined by a third. Two of them hurried past him, while one kept behind.

When Deans left the footpath to cross a road, he saw a green van in the road with its back towards him, while two men were on his right and two on his left-hand side. This was it, he thought.

He crossed the road again, heard footsteps behind him and a voice saying "Right." Then there was a stunning blow on his head, which flung him to the ground. As he lay on the ground, the men beat him unmercifully. He next remembered being flung into a motor van. A hand was placed over his mouth and eyes, and he felt the van moving. A scarf was tied over his eyes, adhesive plaster fixed across his mouth, and his hands and ankles were tied together. His pockets were then rifled and the keys of the bank taken from him.

After some time the van stopped and Sergeant Deans was carried out and thrown onto a pile of snow, face downwards. When he had heard the van drive off, he slowly and painfully got rid of the bandage over his eyes and the gag from his mouth, and kicked his ankles free.

He staggered to a house about 50 yards away, where he was taken in and attended to. He was, as you can imagine, almost in a state of collapse. When the Divisional Surgeon was called, he found Deans suffering from concussion and showing symptoms of exposure to the severe cold of a particularly bitter winter.

A woollen stocking loaded with $3\frac{1}{2}$ pounds of wet sand was found at the scene of the assault—the

weapon with which he had been beaten. He was
off duty for two months.

Meanwhile, however, things had been happening.
The bank at Kentish Town had been watched, and
one of the gang was seen to approach it. He was
arrested, and the keys of the bank and a watch
belonging to Sergeant Deans found on him. Eventually five more men were arrested, and were sentenced in due course to terms of penal servitude
ranging from 3 to 7 years.

15

The Special Branch

AT ABOUT A QUARTER TO FOUR ON THE AFTER-
noon of Friday, December 13, 1867, a barrel of
gunpowder was exploded against the wall of the
exercise yard of the old Clerkenwell House of De-
tention.

A whole street of houses was completely wrecked.
Many innocent people, men, women and children,
were killed or terribly injured.

The perpetrators of this terrible crime were members of the Irish Republican Brotherhood, who believed that by such acts of violence they could
force the British Government to give Ireland Home
Rule. There was at once a nation-wide demand for
their detection and arrest. But how? They worked

under cover, in the utmost secrecy. All the members were sworn under pain of death never to give one another away.

As a result of the Clerkenwell outrage, the plain-clothes force was enlarged, and became a few years later that separate department of the Metropolitan Police known as the C.I.D. But again, in 1884, the Irish dynamiters struck. All over London there were explosions, falling houses, terrible injuries and loss of life. A bomb was exploded in Scotland Yard itself.

The real dangers from these desperate dynamiters were serious enough, but the still small C.I.D. had to cope in addition with a constant stream of alarmist information from frightened citizens. Everyone had seen a bomb, or something that looked like a bomb, or mysterious men with beards and suspicious-looking parcels. In most cases, of course, the mysterious men were perfectly inoffensive people going about their daily work. But each piece of information had to be sifted, just in case there might be something in it which would lead Scotland Yard to the perpetrators of the dynamitings.

To deal with the situation, the C.I.D. set up the Special Branch manned by selected officers of the C.I.D. These were chosen for their fitness in keeping observation on the suspected dynamiters and guarding visiting Royalty, Ministers of the Crown and public buildings.

The Fenian scare lasted only a little while, but in 1887, the year of Queen Victoria's Jubilee, the

Special Branch had a hectic time coping with anarchists who wished to show their disapproval of monarchy by blowing the Queen and all her retinue into smithereens.

There were constant anarchist outbreaks in London and other towns. Small workshops were discovered in which homemade bombs were made. Sometimes the bombs exploded. In February, 1894, an anarchist named Bourdin blew himself to pieces in Greenwich Park with a homemade bomb which he was taking to blow up Greenwich Observatory. Joseph Conrad wrote a thrilling novel about this incident, *The Secret Agent*, which Alfred Hitchcock made into an equally thrilling film.

Many of the anarchists and Irish dynamiters came from abroad (the Irishmen often from America). The Special Branch therefore found it desirable to station some of their men at home and foreign ports, to keep an eye on the movements of foreign conspirators. Their work became so useful that they have been retained at some home ports ever since, and now stand by also at certain airports.

Irish extremists and anarchists were followed by Indian agitators, suffragettes, communists, fascists— all those who seek to overthrow the rule of law for political ends—and on all of them the Special Branch kept a watchful eye.

During the First World War the Special Branch co-operated with the naval and military authorities in spy-catching, and many dramatic interrogations of suspected spies took place in the Assistant Commissioner's room at Scotland Yard. So important, indeed, did the Special Branch's work become that it was for a few years detached from the C.I.D. and placed under an Assistant Commissioner of its own.

Just before the Second World War, the Irish struck yet again. Members of the I.R.A., the Irish Republican Army, deposited homemade bombs in public places, posted them in mailboxes, and killed and injured many innocent people. Thanks to the work of the Special Branch and other officers of the C.I.D., many of these men were rounded up and given long sentences of imprisonment.

The Special Branch, in collaboration with the Intelligence branches of the Services, again played its part in the Second World War, keeping watch on suspected spies and sympathizers with Nazi Germany.

But the day-to-day work of the Special Branch is not spy-catching, nor rounding up dynamiters and other political extremists. Its principal job is that taken over from old John Townsend, the Bow Street runner, of protecting Royalty, Ministers of the Crown or ex-Ministers, distinguished foreign visitors and other public personages who may be exposed to the risk of violence from extremists, or risk of annoyance from harmless lunatics.

The Special Branch also plays an important part in the control of arms, explosives and aliens. The registration, general supervision and deportation of aliens is undertaken by other branches of Scotland Yard, but the Special Branch keeps a watch on those whose activities are unwelcome and carries out the inquiries necessary before an alien is granted British nationality.

As in every branch of the Metropolitan Police, Special Branch men have climbed up the ladder from the beat. But they must have rather different qualifications from those required by other branches of the C.I.D. They must, for instance, have a knowledge of languages. And "information received" plays an even bigger part in certain Special Branch activities than it does in the lives of ordinary C.I.D. officers. So Special Branch men must be especially good at observing while themselves remaining unseen. This merely means that they must dress and conduct themselves in such a way as to blend perfectly with their surroundings.

16

"Dial 999"

"I DON'T KNOW WHAT WE'RE COMING TO," SAID the old police sergeant irritably in 1901, when the first telephone was installed at Scotland Yard. "Why, if this sort of thing goes on, we'll have the public ringing us up direct!"

The other day a member of the public did ring up direct—one of nearly 100,000 amateur detectives who help Scotland Yard every year by dialing 999 and asking for "Police, Scotland Yard." This time it was a lady who had been cleaning her front windows, and had noticed what she thought was a suspicious happening in the street outside. A car had driven up, a man got out of it, took a bundle from the car, crossed the road, entered another car parked there, and drove away. There *might* be nothing in it, the lady said apologetically, but it had seemed rather queer, and she just wondered. . . .

Scotland Yard wondered, too. Had the lady by any chance taken the numbers of the cars? She was a very good detective, and she had. She had written them with her finger in the dirt of the window she was cleaning.

When they heard the numbers, Scotland Yard were more interested than ever, for the first number was that of a car which had just been reported as having been stolen and used for a smash-and-grab raid. The second number was presumably that of the thief's own car. A radio message was sent out to all police cars to look for him, and a few minutes later he was picked up—a very surprised young man—thanks to the quick thinking of the lady window cleaner!

The old sergeant who objected to Scotland Yard's first telephone would no doubt have been shocked

also at members of the public posing as detectives.
There was the 10-year-old Manchester boy who
followed a man escaping from the police for nearly
a mile, and then called to passers-by to stop him.
There was the 14-year-old Cheshire girl who took
a car's number because she noticed its driver glancing constantly and suspiciously in the mirror, and
reported the number to the police, causing the arrest of two men who had stolen over £1,000 worth
of valuables. Amateur detectives such as these would
have shocked the police in the old days. But not
today. All over the country, not only in London,
the 999 system is working many wonders in pre-
venting and detecting crime. Scotland Yard declares
that it is as good as having half a dozen policemen
in every street.

Sometimes the amateur detectives are a little over-
zealous, and there is nothing valuable in the information they telephone to the Yard. But the Yard
doesn't mind that. One 999 call in every 10 leads
to an arrest, and that is a record of which the
public can be very proud.

Not only the public use 999, of course. The policeman on his beat can dial it too. Here is a thrilling example of how it works.

Late one winter's night the Duty Officer of a
division was patrolling in a car not fitted with radio.
He saw three men in a green motor van who were
acting suspiciously. He drove up to them, but they
raced away at terrific speed as soon as they saw

him. The police car gave chase, but as it had no radio, it was not able to report the suspects' movements or ask for help. A uniformed policeman on his beat, however, saw what was happening. He took the license number of the van, dialed 999, and within a few minutes a radio message had gone out warning all police cars in that area to join the chase. Foot police all along the route sent similar messages, and so it was possible for a man in the Information Room at Scotland Yard, 10 miles away, to give almost a running commentary on the chase, directing radio cars on to the trail of the green van wherever it appeared.

In the dark streets of Greenwich, some five miles from where the hue and cry had started, the van was forced to stop. The three men ran in opposite directions, but one of them was caught immediately. The other two disappeared among the murky riverside alleys. But Scotland Yard had not finished with them yet. Three more radio cars were directed to the scene, and their crews, together with local foot police and the men who had already taken part in the chase, threw a cordon round the area and searched it until the two were taken.

Another such exciting chase was set off by a message from a man-in-the-street who kept his wits about him.

At about half-past three one morning, a garage proprietor at Staines, Middlesex, was held up by men in a large black car, who offered him two bottles of rare whisky in exchange for gasoline. He reported to the police; the police telephoned Scotland Yard; and a radio car was told to look for the large black car. It was soon picked up, and the chase began. Up the deserted Great South West Road the two cars sped, at 50, 60, 70 miles an hour. The police car sent radio messages to inform the Yard how the chase was progressing, and two more cars were directed to race ahead of the black car and cut it off.

With the police hot on their trail, the crooks tried to defend themselves. Hurtling along at 70 miles an hour, they began hurling bottles of whisky at the car behind. Glass crashed and splintered on the road in front of the police car's tires, but it kept on. Two dozen bottles exploded about the police—but the crooks could not get away. At last their car crashed into a lorry, the pursuing police cars drew up, and every single man was arrested. The black car, of course, had been stolen, and used to raid the cellars of a country club.

In Charing Cross Road one night, the passengers of a "wanted" car were being interrogated when the driver slipped in his clutch and away he went. A member of the police car crew jumped on to the running board and hung on desperately. The crooks' car charged a safety zone and tried to catch the policeman between the car and the concrete post, but still, though badly hurt, he kept his hold. Raining blows on him, the crooks at last forced him off. Nevertheless, he had delayed them long enough to let the police car catch up, force the passengers of the wanted car to stop, and arrest them.

"One chap I chased," said the driver of crime car 5D, "scuttled down a pitch-black alley. I couldn't see a thing, and of course in the excitement I'd left my torch in the car. I knew he was trapped, because there was no way out, but I just couldn't see him at all in the darkness."

"What did you do?" the policeman was asked.

"Went down after him, of course," he replied, slightly surprised that he should have been asked.

Put yourself in that policeman's place for a moment. Down a dark alley after a man you cannot see. He may have a gun, brass knuckles or a razor, and he may be desperate enough to use them without mercy. You have nothing but your bare hands. There's no reason why you should go on. It's very easy to return to the car and say, "Chummy got away." No one can call you a liar or a coward if you do. But you do go on, because you have the honor to belong to the police force where such things are done every day, and because it is your job to prevent decent people being preyed upon by rogues.

But once again we must come back to the machine behind the men, for without the whole machine of the police force, individual courage is often in vain. A visit to the Information Room at Scotland Yard is enlightening, for there one can see how the system of radio communication is organized to cover the 734 square miles of the Metropolitan Police area.

There is a big underground room, below street level, with smaller rooms opening from it. The walls are painted green and white, there are green tubular chairs, and "daylight" lighting which gives an impression of super-efficient modernity.

At one end of the room is the corner to which all Scotland Yard 999 calls come direct.

The operators, uniformed policemen with more than 10 years' service, are especially experienced in dealing with agitated old ladies who think they have burglars under the bed, with people who may be still dizzy from a housebreaker's blackjack, and with the many others who for one reason or another cannot tell their stories clearly and concisely.

Sometimes, all the operator has to go on is a scream. Then he must get the switchboard to trace where the call came from, and send police cars speeding to the scene of what may be murder—or some drunken man taking it out on his wife with a belt-end on a Saturday night.

Normally, the operator extracts the caller's story: the address at which police assistance is wanted, and what the trouble is. He writes it on a pad with two carbon copies. One of these copies goes to the Information Room's "loggist," who checks that the information has not been previously received, and files the copy for future reference. A second copy goes to the teleprinter room opening off the Information Room, from which crime bulletins are teleprinted direct to 97 police stations in the London area at 15 minutes past every hour.

The operator takes the third copy of the message across to four big tables in the middle of the room, on which are large-scale maps of the four police districts. On these tables are little counters, each of which represents a radio vehicle or motor-launch. A round counter represents a radio crime car. A triangle represents one of 32 Traffic and Accident Group ("TAG") cars, each with its two attendant motor cyclists. There are 16 little boat-shaped counters, representing Thames Division launches. And there are 23 square counters representing "Q" cars, which look like ordinary civilian cars and are manned by plain-clothes policemen.

The operator looks at these tables, selects the proper car nearest to the scene of the incident, and places a red ring around the token to show that the car is now engaged. Then he writes on the message the car's code number—5D, for instance—and hands the message to another policeman who sits in front of a silver-colored microphone.

Within a minute or two of the telephone call having been received, the announcer at the microphone is saying, "Hallo, 5D from M2GW. Message from Information Room begins. . . ."

And in 5D, two miles away, the car's observer takes down the message. There is a brief discussion of the quickest way to reach the spot, then the driver steps on the accelerator and is away.

They will tell you in Information Room that they will have a car on the scene, if it is in inner London, within three minutes of the radio message being sent. In the bigger areas of outer London, of course, it takes a little longer. But not always. A TAG car in Kingston, for instance, was halted at some traffic lights when an all-cars message came through to look for a stolen vehicle. The observer jotted down the number, looked up and said, "Blimey, there he is!" The stolen car was coming towards them from the opposite direction. They turned their car, chased him, and pulled him in. The owner of the stolen car had dialed 999 scarcely 10 minutes before!

With crooks using fast cars which may be in London at midnight and a hundred miles away two hours later, radio, telephone and teleprinter are essential if police forces in different parts of the country are to co-operate in defeating them.

One night St. Albans police telephoned Information Room. St. Albans is not in the Metropolitan Police area, but no crook can feel that he is safe just because he has crossed the imaginary line dividing one police force from another. On this particular night a St. Albans constable on his beat had noticed a car behaving suspiciously. It was only suspicion—but the car *might* have been used in housebreaking. From Information Room the message went out to all cars, to look for this suspicious fellow and try to find out what he was up to. This throws a great responsibility on the crime car men, because such a very slender thread of suspicion does not warrant an arrest.

In this particular case, however, the crime cars were not called on, for the car was found abandoned in the St. Albans area a short time after the call had gone out. It *had* been used in a housebreaking. And it had a London number plate. Another message to Information Room: would the C.I.D. find out who the car's owner was?

Within a short time the C.I.D. had traced the car-hire firm that owned the car. This firm said it had hired the car the night before to a couple of men whom we will call Smith and Brown.

Another call to the Yard. Anything known by C.R.O. about Smith and Brown? Yes, C.R.O. knew far too much about them, including their addresses.

Mr. Smith was sitting down to what he no doubt thought was a well-earned breakfast when the C.I.D. called upon him. Mr. Brown, however, considered himself rather clever. *He* had gone to a London police station, and reported that the car which he had hired the night before had been stolen by nasty criminals, and would Scotland Yard please get it back for him.

Unfortunately for Mr. Brown, Scotland Yard had been slightly more clever, for they had anticipated this alibi of his. So they had sent a message to all police stations giving instructions that if Mr. Brown called with such a story, he was to be detained. As his alibi did not stand very close examination, he was arrested.

In a small room next door to the Information Room, and part of the Yard's widely flung communications system, sits a man listening in to Paris, Czechoslovakia, Denmark, Finland, Germany, Holland, Italy, Luxemburg, Portugal, Sweden, Switzerland.

He is the British link in the chain of wireless communication between all those national police forces represented in the International Criminal Police Commission.

The Central Bureau of the I.C.P.C. is in Paris, and all contributing governments have agreed to an exchange of information affecting each other's criminals. Many European records were destroyed during the Second World War by the Germans, and the British records were extremely useful to draw upon. Now, as national police forces return to normal, the exchange is just as useful to the British. If John Brown of Liverpool is arrested for a crime in Prague, Scotland Yard's C.R.O. file on John Brown will be asked for, and sent. If Jean LeBrun transfers his swindling activities from the French Riviera to Liverpool, everything that the French police have on Jean LeBrun is at the disposal of their British colleagues.

All the information which comes over the I.C.P.C.

wireless link comes in Morse. Morse is an international language. The message may be sent out in German or Swedish, but the man beside the wireless set at Scotland Yard can take it down in dots and dashes without knowing a word of the language. When he has taken it down, it is passed to the language experts of Special Branch for translation, then goes to Central Office. The men there are responsible for action taken in most I.C.P.C. cases.

The international wireless link is very useful and devastatingly quick in its results. One day, for instance, Paris came through. A man boarding a French plane for Heath Row airport was suspected of having in his possession many thousands of pounds' worth of smuggled nylons and jewelry. The information was flashed to Heath Row, and that particular traveler met a very inquisitive group of customs men and police officers on his arrival.

The modern criminal can use fast cars or airplanes to operate across county or international boundaries. But the police, with the help of 999, radio cars and the international wireless link, operate just a little bit faster.

17

The River Police

FROM DARTFORD TO TEDDINGTON, A DISTANCE OF 36 miles, the river Thames is patrolled night and day by launches of the Metropolitan Police's Thames Division.

In 1873 Thames Division acquired its own C.I.D. officers, and twelve years later three steam pinnaces were added to the fleet of rowing boats. New police stations were opened, including that at Waterloo Pier, which is the only floating police station in the world.

Then came the introduction of motor boats, and with them new duties—first aid to the injured, artificial respiration to people rescued from the water, the task of securing drifting craft. Rocket lifesaving apparatus, up-to-date first-aid appliances, salvage gear, fire-fighting equipment, two-way radio telephony, have all helped the Thames Divison to make the Thames more and more secure for the men and ships which ply upon it. In 1797, before the Thames Police were founded, losses on the river totaled £506,000. In 1947, when the Thames Division proudly celebrated 150 years of service, losses were £2,003 10s. 2½d.!

With the Second World War there opened a

glorious chapter in the history of the guardians of London's river. When the bombing of London began, the Thames Police found themselves in the very front line. Wharves and ships burst into flames, blazing barges broke loose from their moorings and went swinging down the Thames, only to return, still blazing, on the tide; people were driven from their riverside houses and patients from a riverside hospital, with no way of escape by land. The first night of the blitz was spent quenching fires, rescuing stranded people and shepherding burning barges to places of safety.

As the blitz continued, the Thames policeman's daily life, and especially his night duty, was seldom free from danger. Mines were a special problem. Indicators were fitted at stations for observation purposes, and men on patrol kept constant watch.

To many Thames policemen, perhaps the most dramatic sight of the war was in May and June, 1940, when the unforgettable armada of yachts and small craft from the upper reaches of the Thames made their way down river to cross the Channel and to play their historic part in the evacuation of Dunkirk. There was bitter disappointment when it was decided that Thames Division men could not be allowed to join the great expedition.

Today, with ever more up-to-date equipment, the Thames Division continues its task of guarding London's river. Repairs to boats and equipment are carried out in the Division's own Wapping repair shops and boatyard, to which a floating dock was added in 1946.

The newest addition to the fleet of the Thames Division is a small craft especially built and equipped for use in dragging. Dragging and recovery of articles from the Thames and other inland waterways has always been a feature of Thames Police work, but when they were called to help land divisions, there was always difficulty in transporting heavy boats and equipment overland. So a flat-bottomed boat was built, light and easily lifted and carried by a crew of three. When it is needed, this boat with its equipment is loaded into a standard police tender, into which it fits neatly, and is driven with its crew to the scene of operations. The dragging equipment consists of permanent magnets for recovering metal objects like firearms, ammunition, jemmies; steel drags for bodies or articles enclosed in sacks; a 16-feet pole drag fitted with a three-pronged grapnel for use in lifting articles when found; first-aid equipment for use in emergency.

So when someone suspects that the stolen Coronation Stone has been dumped in the Serpentine in Hyde Park, it is men of the Thames Division, with their drags worked from this special boat, who are called in to bring a huge stone to the surface.

They drag for many other things, too. One night some people in a pub on the outskirts of London heard a car being driven down a lane outside, which led nowhere except to some disused gravel pits. The car didn't come back; and talking the thing over among themselves, the pub customers decided to tell the police. Next morning the police inspected the gravel pits, and on the margin of one of them found tire marks. There was also a film of oil on the surface of the water which, in places, was 80 feet deep.

The Thames Division men were sent for, and with their magnetic drags they found the car in about 14 feet of water. They passed wires under it, attached the ends of the wires to a bulldozer on shore, and soon had the car out again.

It was a car which had been reported as stolen from the West End of London a few days before, but the owner didn't seem quite as pleased to get it back as the police thought he would be. In fact, when they began to make inquiries, they found that he had paid someone to drive the car into that gravel pit, hoping it would never be found, and had claimed the insurance money on it. Instead of the money, however, he got 9 months' imprisonment.

The first time magnetic drags were used was in October, 1945. Early one morning a taxi driver, Frank Everitt, nicknamed "The Duke," was found shot through the head in a firewatcher's shelter on Lambeth Bridge. The Chief Superintendent of the Flying Squad took charge of the case, and his inquiries led him to believe that the revolver with which The Duke had been shot had been thrown into the Thames from Lambeth Bridge.

So the Thames Division got to work with electromagnetic drags, capable of lifting 56 pounds weight, the electricity for which was supplied from accumulators in the drag-boat.

They dragged for that gun for six days. They found a great many interesting things, but no gun. Officially, the murderers of The Duke were never found, and the case is still, as they say, open.

A case with a more satisfactory official ending came while the search for that gun was still going on. A Polish airman was found shot through the heart on Westminster Bridge late one November night. It was suspected that Poles were mixed up in the affair of The Duke, and it seemed distinctly possible that this Pole, too, had been murdered. Once more the magnetic drags were set to work to find the gun. They got between two and three hundredweights of assorted old metal, including some safes, nuts, bolts, a car starting handle—and three guns.

It was established that the fatal shot had been fired from one of these, and as a result of this, and other inquiries made by the C.I.D. into the dead man's past life, the coroner was satisfied that the Pole had committed suicide.

Such events are exciting, but they do not happen every day. The Thames Division's main task, like that of the uniformed men on shore, is in keeping the river free from crime. There are no thrilling chases after smugglers at 25 knots. Those, if and when they happen, are the job of the Customs launches, though of course the Thames police will give any help they are asked for.

But who would say that chasing smugglers is more important than giving the alarm which eventually prevents a valuable cargo from being burned? Or being on the spot when towed barges come adrift and the Thames men find themselves wrestling with icy tow ropes—generally at night—to get a barge under control before it hits a bridge?

One Thames sergeant was tackling a barge like that in a thick fog when his foot slipped on the ice, and he found himself in the bitter cold water. He managed to grab hold of a plank, and shouted, but it was three-quarters of an hour before his crew found him. It was, he told me, the longest three-quarters of an hour of his life, and he had almost given up life and hope when he was dragged out.

Such incidents make no newspaper headlines and win no medals. They are just a part of the job which goes on 24 hours a day, 365 days in the year, and without which the Thames would become once more the haunt of river pirates and scuffle hunters as it was in the old days before the Thames police were founded.

The men of the Thames Division have all served their time on the beat, and some of them have had Royal Navy or Merchant Navy experience before they joined the force. But all that Thames Division asks of its volunteers is that they shall be able to handle a small boat. The chief inspector in charge of the station at Waterloo Pier first learned to handle small boats as a lad on the Serpentine, and the lakes in London and provincial parks have probably given as many men to the Division as the Navy. After all, you don't learn much about handling a launch in a choppy river from having once served on a 20,000-ton battleship!

But whether they come from the Serpentine or H.M.S. *Vanguard*, there is something indescribable about the Thames men which stamps them at once as different from their comrades on land. They seem more weather-beaten, wrapped up in their great frieze coats; their eyes are narrowed against the cutting wind; and they walk even on land as if they were on hair-trigger springs balanced against the sudden lurch of a police launch in a tug's backwash.

It is a tough life on the river, for tough men, but it is a good life. "Dawn on a July morning," mused the chief inspector. "The river all to yourself. The sun just coming up behind the wharves and offices. *Then* you feel absolutely on top of the world."

18

Horses and Dogs

WHAT THE MICROSCOPE IS TO THE HEAD OF THE Laboratory, Rajah's nose is to Rajah.

Rajah is a detective in his own right, a police dog, a big Alsatian with an alert, friendly face.

He is not friendly, however, if you have been doing what you shouldn't do. He recently went on patrol in Hyde Park with his master—the uniformed policeman who was trained with him and who alone can handle him—two more policemen, and another dog. The patrol spotted a gang of 19 young roughnecks who had been deliberately smashing park chairs and making a general nuisance of themselves. They ran away when they saw the police, but Rajah and the other dog, who can run faster than any mere human, soon caught up with them. One of the gang rashly tried to throw Rajah into the Serpentine, whereupon Rajah provided a mild sample of his fighting qualities, and the rest of the gang decided it would be wiser to come quietly.

But Rajah will fight only if the chap he is after attacks him first. He, and all other police dogs, are taught to tackle a crook's right arm. Most people are right-handed, and it is wise to immobilize that dangerous right arm first. But Rajah will not bite it. He will not even tear the sleeve. He will just grasp the arm gently with his teeth, and if the wanted man stops and stands still, Rajah is satisfied. As long as the man remains quiet, Rajah will stay quiet too, waiting for his handler to come up and deal with the situation. But Rajah will not leave that man until his master does arrive. If the man climbs a tree or dives into a building, Rajah will wait there on guard. After a really long cross-country trail— and it takes a great deal to throw Rajah off the scent—he will wait for an hour, for two hours if necessary, patiently, quietly—and utterly remorselessly.

Criminals do not like the dogs, which cannot be evaded as easily as men. Give Rajah a fair scent to follow, and he will not leave it until he finds the man the scent belongs to. He will follow for an hour, for four hours, for eight hours if necessary, padding along at the full stretch of the long white tracking lead, dragging his master hot-foot after him.

A housebreaker was chased through dark streets at two o'clock in the morning by foot police and radio cars, until he took refuge in the huge garden of a big house. To find him, with no light but that of torches, would have taken many hours, and during the search the crook would have had a fair chance of escape. So the police didn't try to find him. They stood on guard outside, and one of the crime cars asked Information Room by radio for a dog.

Most divisions now have dogs, but a few have not and draw from a central district "pool" at which there are always dogs and handlers instantly available to go by car to any place they are wanted.

In this particular case, a dog arrived within a very short time, was put on the trail, and took the police straight to the housebreaker's hiding place.

Dogs are especially useful, of course, for patrolling parks, commons and other open spaces where modern Jack Sheppards are sometimes tempted to try snatching purses from defenceless women. However, the modern Jack Sheppard does not like being chased for a mile in the dark over gorse bushes, ditches and sandpits by a kind of Hound of the Baskervilles, and he is becoming cautious about where he does his purse-snatching.

But the dogs have other uses than thief-taking. They will track lost children, for instance, and recently Rajah was put on to the trail of a man who had left home threatening to commit suicide. Rajah and his master spent eight hours on that search, and found the man at last, too; but they were too late to prevent his achieving his purpose.

Although dogs had been used by the police in exceptional cases since 1888, Scotland Yard began training its own dogs in 1946, when six Labrador retrievers were taken on. The Labrador is a good tracker, and a powerful, heavy dog for detaining criminals. But like some human beings, he does not much care for work after dark, so the Yard began to acquire Alsatians, which are as keen, alert and intelligent at three o'clock on a cold, wet morning as on the hottest summer day.

Some of the dogs have been given to the Yard at ages varying from three to fifteen months. After 15 months, they are too old to train properly. Training takes three months, and is done at the kennels at Imber Court, Thames Ditton. The officer in charge has done his time on the beat and as a uniformed sergeant. He has always loved and understood dogs, bred pedigrees in his spare time, and when Scotland Yard wanted a "dog man," applied eagerly for the job of his dreams.

Master and dog are trained together. The handlers, all uniformed men, volunteer for the duty, and as dogs become available the men who will handle them are sent by their divisions to study at Imber Court. It is here they learn to know their dogs, and the dogs learn to know and trust them. Man and dog together learn the words of command, whistles and gestures with which the dog is controlled at long or short range. The dog will obey no signals except those of his master, whom he worships. Woe betide any foolish man who tries to beat up that master in sight of the dog, for he will quickly have a hefty Alsatian with powerful jaws and sharp teeth on top of him.

When the training is finished, the dog goes to live with his master, a kennel and food being provided at the master's home. Once a fortnight master and dog come back to Imber Court for a refresher course, because working constantly in city streets, with their confused noises and smells, tends to blunt the dog's sensibilities.

Dogs are Scotland Yard's newest animal allies. But Imber Court also houses the headquarters of the oldest, the superb horses of the Mounted Branch. There the Chief Superintendent of the Mounted Branch directs his 200 horses and 200 men for the special duties which only they can undertake.

The horses come to Imber Court as unbroken 3-year-olds, mostly from Yorkshire. They are first broken in to bit and saddle, then accustomed gradually to the sudden noises and roars of traffic which make most highly bred horses behave like rodeo broncos.

This training is done in rather an interesting way. The young horses, mounted by their riders, stand in a circle. The Chief Superintendent waves flags in their faces, or sounds a firebell or an enormous and raucous rattle. But while he does this, another man goes around giving each horse a handful of oats, so that instead of associating these noises with something horrible, the horses associate it with something especially nice. One false or hasty step at this stage in their training, and they will be finished as police horses, for they will dread noises or sudden movement, and will shy their rider out of the saddle at a dropped newspaper or a back-firing bus. But the trainers at Imber Court know horses, and the false step is never taken.

A Metropolitan Police horse, when he is posted from the Mounted school to the division where he will serve, will "take" almost anything. An old constable of the Mounted Branch told me that he was riding one day along a road which was under repair. As he approached, he saw four laborers with massive electric drills wink at each other and make gestures in his direction. Then they stood in line, motionless as guardsmen, with their backs towards him, while the foreman watched. As the Mounted man came abreast of the laborers, the foreman gave a signal and the four electric drills erupted in an earth-shaking roar which it was hoped would cause the horse to throw its rider. But the horse never batted an eyelid, and five very disappointed men were left watching that Mounted policeman's triumphant smile.

The old duties of the Mounted Branch, taken over from the Horse Patrols, are now performed by crime and traffic wireless cars. But the Mounted men are unsurpassed in shepherding and marshaling large crowds or processions.

For this reason there will always be a Mounted Branch, no matter how many sleek cars Scotland Yard acquires. The men, carefully chosen from the ranks of the foot police, have in the past generally learned to ride in the cavalry before they join the force. Now the Army has almost lost its cavalry, but a man of not too heavy build can be turned into a first-rate Mounted policeman after six months at Imber Court. And there is never any lack of volunteers!

19

At the Scene of the Crime

IN CHAPTER FIVE WE DESCRIBED SCOTLAND YARD as a machine, consisting of interlocking parts, each with a particular job to do in making the machine run smoothly. In previous chapters we have taken the machine to pieces and looked at the parts separately. Now we are putting it together again, and you will see in this and the next chapter how all the parts fit in—the policeman on his beat, the gun expert and laboratory scientists, the fingerprint and photography men, C.R.O. and detectives of the C.I.D., the man-in-the-street and the newspapers, those vital links between police and public—to detect the perpetrators of a murder.

At about 2:30 p.m. on April 29th, 1947, three young men wearing masks and armed with revolvers entered a jeweler's shop in the West End of London. Two men came in by the side entrance, while a third entered through the main shop door.

One of the men from the side entrance jumped over the counter, threatened an assistant and a customer with his revolver, and demanded the keys of the safe. The assistant refused, whereupon he was beaten on the head with a revolver.

Hearing this commotion, the man who had come

in through the main door fired a bullet through the communicating door between the main shop and the inner department. Fortunately he hit no one—but the bullet lodged in a wooden panel of the shop.

A general fight then took place, and the three men, becoming frightened at the bravery of the staff, ran out of the shop by the side door. One of them left a small revolver on the counter.

They ran from the shop into a busy London street, with dozens of people going about their daily business. The three men jumped into a motor car which they had previously stolen, and which they had left outside the shop door. The car would not start, so they hurriedly abandoned the vehicle and ran away together.

By this time the hue and cry was after them. The assistant who had been beaten in the shop staggered to the side door and raised an alarm, which was taken up by people in the street.

A man named Alec d'Antiquis was riding a motor-cycle down the street. He apparently heard the shouts, saw three men running toward him down the middle of the road, and switching off his engine, skidded the motocycle broadside across their path.

One of the men thereupon shot him at point-blank range through the temple. D'Antiquis slumped off his machine into the gutter, and the motorcycle slowly toppled over on top of him, as a horror-stricken crowd gathered. He died later in the hospital.

After the shooting, the gunmen separated. The

man who had fired the fatal shot scurried off in one direction and was soon lost to view. His two accomplices kept together, and two brave passers-by, though they had seen the fate of Alec d'Antiquis, tackled them. They managed to trip one of the gunmen and make him drop his revolver. They grabbed him, but the gunman kicked and fought like a demon, causing them to lose their grip. He picked up the gun from the roadway and threatened them with it. Then, as the passers-by hesitated, the two criminals made off into busy Tottenham Court Road, and disappeared among the traffic.

Meanwhile, someone had dialed 999, police had appeared, and the street was cordoned off.

You would think that a crime committed in broad daylight, before a street full of people, would be easily solved. Statements were taken from 23 people who had been more or less eye-witnesses of the murder. Scarcely any of those 23 descriptions of the murderers were the same!

Experts from the Finger Print Branch and the Photographic Section carefully examined every inch of the shop and the abandoned car. They found fingerprints in plenty, but most of these could be identified as those of the shop assistants or the car's rightful owner.

The revolver left behind in the shop and the bullet which had been fired there were taken to Mr. Robert Churchill, the gun expert. He found that the bullet had been fired from a .45 Colt revolver, and that the revolver found in the shop was not the weapon concerned. On the following day, the fatal bullet was taken from Alec d'Antiquis' head by Sir Bernard Spilsbury and handed over to Mr. Churchill. This was found to have been fired from a .32 revolver. The two bullets—one a .32 and the other a .45—remained, of course, in the possession of the police.

The evening and morning newspapers printed many columns about the murder, appealing to anyone who had information which might be valuable to get in touch with Scotland Yard. Hundreds of people came forward, the C.I.D. officers worked day and night interviewing them, sifting the information received, making the inquiries arising from it.

Among the members of the public who came forward with information was a very apologetic taxi-cab driver, who "didn't think there was anything in his story," but felt in duty bound to tell it.

He said that on the fatal afternoon he was driving his cab, with a passenger in it, when a man wearing a scarf jumped on the running board and tried to hire him. When the man saw that there was already a passenger in the cab, he jumped off. The cab driver had noticed that the man ran across the road and joined another young man who was standing at the entrance to a block of offices, about a quarter of a mile from the scene of the murder.

Now you must remember that this story was only one among the hundreds told to police officers, and that every one of those hundreds of stories which had any substance in it was being checked. At the same time Mr. Robert Churchill was working on the gun, the fingerprint men were going over the shop inch by inch in search of fingerprints, detectives of the C.I.D. were sounding all their sources of "information received" for any clues, and C.R.O. were looking in their records for likely perpetrators of armed robberies. They were paying particular attention, in view of the youth of the murderers, to men recently released or escaped from penal institutions.

When the taxi driver's story came in, it seemed on the surface just another story, just another faint hope of a trail. In the course of routine inquiries detectives went to the block of offices where the two young men had been seen. They asked everyone there if they had noticed these two young men.

Two people had seen them: a young office boy, and the driver of a lorry who had been delivering goods. Between them, they recalled that one of the two men was wearing a raincoat, a cap and a white scarf when he entered the offices, but when he left, some few minutes afterwards, he was not wearing these things.

Then detectives searched the premises from top to bottom. On the fourth floor of the building, hidden behind a dusty and disused counter in a storeroom, they found a scarf, folded in a triangle and knotted, a cap, and a raincoat.

These were rushed to the Laboratory and carefully

examined. The maker's tab had been removed from the lining at the neck of the coat, but Scotland Yard are not content to examine just the outside of any garment which comes into their hands. They took this coat to pieces. Sewn in the seam near the right-hand pocket, between the lining and outer material, they found a linen stock ticket bearing the name of a tailor with hundreds of branches all over the country. They realized that in the course of a year these branches probably sell hundreds of coats such as this. But it was their first definite clue.

Detectives took the ticket to Leeds, to the factory where the coat had been made. From other markings on the ticket, the Leeds factory manager was able to say that this particular coat must have been sold at one of three branch shops.

Two of the three branch shops mentioned were in suburban districts of London, and inquiries were made there first. Yes, they had sold raincoats of that type. Yes, they could give the names and addresses of several buyers, for those were the days of clothing coupons . . . of *forged* clothing coupons . . . and shop assistants had got into the habit of jotting down a customer's name and address, just in case the coupons he surrendered turned out to be forgeries.

So detectives went to work on that list of names and addresses. There would be a knock on some suburban door.

"Good evening, sir. I am a police officer. I believe you bought a raincoat recently. Could you tell me if the coat is still in your possession?"

The householder would be slightly puzzled, perhaps slightly resentful. "Well, yes, if you really want to know, it is," he would say. "In fact it's hanging up here. Want to look at it?"

"If you wouldn't mind, sir."

A quick look would be taken to make sure that it really *was* there.

Then, of course, the householder would want to ask questions. What was this all about? Was his caller really a detective? It must be awfully exciting to be a detective, investigating murders and things. . . .

After a few hours of this fruitless search and polite chat, the detective would sigh and wonder if it really is so exciting being a detective, and if it wouldn't be nicer to be sitting in front of a warm fire reading a detective story!

In time that particular list of addresses had been covered and all the raincoats accounted for. Now on to the next shop.

That shop was in Deptford. And that shop *had* sold the coat to a man with an address in Deptford.

The address given was a large block of flats. The detective, of course, did not go straight along to that address. He wanted to find out a little about the man first. So he made inquiries at the little shop on the corner, in the café, inquiries of the old lady hanging out the wash on the fourth floor. But no one knew of the man in those flats. What, he was not at Number 160? Who did live there then?

"Oh, it's Mr. —— you want. Oh, now you come to speak of it, I believe —— *is* his Christian name. Funny mistake to make."

More inquiries. Anything known about the owner of the raincoat? Yes, he went into the local pub every Sunday noon, regular as clockwork. He was related to a man named Jenkins . . .

Jenkins . . . Jenkins . . . Wasn't there a Jenkins on a C.R.O. card? Let's have a look. Harry Jenkins, just out of Borstal. Living in Bermondsey. Elder brother doing eight years for manslaughter following a smash and grab raid on a jeweler's shop. . . .

On Sunday morning, May 11th, twelve days after Alec d'Antiquis' death, plainclothes detectives inconspicuously mounted guard outside the address of Harry Jenkins' sister and brother-in-law. At 11:45 a man came out for his Sunday morning constitutional, and a shadow tailed off after him.

Five minutes later Jenkins's sister was being confronted with the fatal raincoat. Was it her husband's? Well, it *looked* like her husband's. He had lost his in a public house off Tottenham Court Road about five weeks previously. It might be her husband's, but she couldn't definitely say. She was agitated; but in reply to further questions she would say no more. The detectives left, and five minutes later the woman left, too. A shadow peeled off after her. She hurried to an address in Bermondsey, the address in C.R.O.'s records of Harry Jenkins, the address of her brother. . . .

At 2 o'clock that day Jenkins's brother-in-law was invited to visit the local police station. Had he bought a raincoat fairly recently? Yes, he had, he admitted readily. Was this it? He tried it on. Yes, it seemed to be. How had it gone out of his possession? he was asked. Why, he'd left it in a cinema some weeks previously, he replied. Then why had his wife said that it had been stolen from a public house in the Tottenham Court Road, near where Alec d'Antiquis had been murdered?

He considered this for a few minutes. Then he confessed that neither story was true. His wife had told him that she had lent it to her brother Harry.

Harry Jenkins. . . .

In a short time police officers were knocking on Harry Jenkins's door. . . .

20

Inquiries by the Yard

ON THE DAY BEFORE HARRY JENKINS WAS TAKEN to Tottenham Court Road police station for questioning, a seven-year-old boy was playing on the foreshore of the river Thames at Wapping, when he noticed something lying in the mud. He picked it up. It was a loaded .32 revolver, from which one bullet had been fired. It was taken to Mr. Robert Churchill for his expert examination, and he quickly established that it was the gun with which Alec d'Antiquis had been shot.

The point at which the gun had been found was within a quarter of a mile of the block of flats in which lived the parents of Harry Jenkins's wife.

Harry Jenkins again. . . .

But the police will tell you that there is a very considerable difference between being absolutely sure in your own mind who committed a certain crime, and being able to prove it to a British judge and jury in a court of law.

Besides, the police wanted not one man, but three. They had a long way to go yet.

Among the associates of Harry Jenkins were a young man named Christopher Geraghty, aged 21, and a youth of 17, Terence Rolt. Both were asked to account for their movements on April 29th. Geraghty said that he was at home in bed, suffering from boils. Rolt said that he stayed in bed most of the day. Their mothers confirmed these stories. When the young men were told that Jenkins had been detained, they became very agitated. But agitation is not evidence, and they were allowed to go.

Harry Jenkins was lined up for identification by 27 people who had been in the street when Alec d'Antiquis was shot. With him in the line-up were about a dozen other men of similar build. Not one of the witnesses picked out Jenkins.

Before the line-up, Jenkins saw the chief inspector from Central Office who was in charge of the case and said, "I shouldn't be picked out, and if you play fair I'll tell you something interesting afterwards."

After the line-up, he and his sister saw the chief inspector again. Jenkins turned to his sister, and said, "Tell him who I lent the coat to."

His sister said, "Bill Walsh."

Jenkins hurriedly added, "We saw him about a fortnight ago in Southend. He's knocking around with a blonde girl who works in a café. If you go to Southend, go to No. 32; I don't know the name of the road."

Bill Walsh was identified from C.R.O. as a convict on parole who had failed to report to the police in accordance with the provisions of his parole.

But the chief inspector was interested in what Jenkins had said for quite another reason. Jenkins had the reputation of being extraordinarily loyal to his associates. When he had first been brought in for questioning, he had refused to say anything. Now that the witnesses at the line-up had failed to identify him, there was no evidence available against him at the moment, and he would normally have been allowed to go. Yet at this moment, when it must have seemed to him that the case against him had collapsed, he had chosen to break his own code of loyalty, and had put the police on the trail of one of his friends.

The chief inspector, of course, said nothing about all this to Jenkins. He merely made a mental note to find out somehow *why* Jenkins had mentioned Walsh.

And he went to Southend.

At Southend Police Station, he faced an immense task. Every policeman on his beat carries a little notebook, and in this notebook he records *everything* which happens while he is on duty. A stray dog. A wallet found in the street. A man behaving suspiciously. A driver warned for parking in the wrong place. All very trivial, you may think. But think again. Those little notebooks contain a complete record of what was going on in a town at any given moment.

Every single one of those notebooks was brought to the chief inspector, and he went carefully through them. He found two entries which interested him. At about 9:40 p.m. on April 25th, reported one police constable, he had noticed two young men behaving suspiciously in a telephone kiosk. They gave their names as Christopher James Geraghty and Michael Joseph Gillam. And at 7:15 a.m. on April 26th, another police constable had been informed by a member of the public that there was a .45 revolver lying in the shrubbery near the pier. The policeman had taken the gun, fully loaded, to the police station.

When he had finished with the notebooks, the chief inspector was able to trace the father of the girl with whom Jenkins said Bill Walsh had been "knocking around," and the father had an interesting story to tell. He said that Walsh and Jenkins were at Southend on April 25th, and that during the evening Walsh for no apparent reason left the company. When Jenkins heard of this, the father went on, he said that Walsh had double-crossed him, and he would have his revenge.

So here was the motive behind Jenkins's apparent betrayal of Walsh to the police!

But Walsh was not finished with yet. Because he had been friendly with several people in Southend, all these people were visited, and their houses searched. At one house were two watches which had been given to the occupant by Walsh. The occupant said that he believed these watches were the proceeds of an armed hold-up at a jeweler's shop in Bayswater, London, on the early afternoon of April 25th, four days before the d'Antiquis murder.

At once Mr. Walsh became a very much wanted man. His description was published in the newspapers, and police everywhere were informed through the *Police Gazette* and other C.R.O. publications that he was wanted for questioning.

But though the hue and cry might now be out after Walsh, though Walsh might very well prove to be one of the three gunmen in the d'Antiquis murder, the police were still interested in Jenkins, Geraghty and Rolt. They were shadowed, and detectives reported that they had met in a public house at Clerkenwell, and appeared to be "on edge."

On May 16th, a Mr. Morris, an ex-detective

sergeant of the C.I.D. who during his service had had Walsh on his hands and had read in the papers that Walsh was wanted, saw him walking along the street. Mr. Morris detained him.

Walsh was then questioned, and after he had been cautioned, he made a statement. He denied having borrowed a raincoat from Harry Jenkins. He denied that he had any active hand in the d'Antiquis crime, although he admitted discussing the hold-up and reconnoitering the neighborhood with Jenkins, Geraghty and another man, who subsequently withdrew from the plan. He also described a man named "Joe," who lived at Kilburn and was associated with Jenkins and Geraghty. He made a complete confession about the Bayswater hold-up. He, Geraghty, Jenkins and "Joe" had got away with £5,000-worth of jewelry from the Bayswater shop. He and Jenkins had taken the loot to Southend, where he had double-crossed Jenkins and slipped away with the whole proceeds.

This ends Walsh's part in the story of the d'Antiquis murder, except that he and "Joe"—who was identified as Michael Joseph Gillam—were sentenced to five years' penal servitude apiece for their part in the Bayswater hold-up.

But though Walsh was in a sense a red herring drawn across the trail of the d'Antiquis murderers, he had given the police the handle they were seeking against Jenkins, Geraghty and Rolt.

Geraghty was pulled in for questioning, confronted with Walsh's statement about the Bayswater hold-up, and with the .45 revolver found in the shrubbery at Southend. He admitted his complicity in that affair, and acknowledged that the Southend revolver was his. He was then asked to make a statement about the d'Antiquis murder, and finally agreed. In this statement he implicated Rolt, but not Jenkins— Jenkins was a close friend of his, and Jenkins and Geraghty had sworn never to betray each other.

Now it was Rolt's turn. He had sworn no such oath of brotherhood as Geraghty, and he mentioned Jenkins by name. Jenkins was then arrested, and the three were charged with the murder of Alec d'Antiquis and assault at the jeweler's.

Meanwhile, one further piece of evidence had come to light. Another boy was exploring the Thames foreshore within 50 yards of where the first boy had found the .32 revolver. This boy also found a gun, a .45, and Mr. Robert Churchill was able to establish that this was the revolver from which the shot had been fired in the jeweler's shop.

The case was complete. Jenkins and Geraghty were sentenced to death, and Rolt, being under 18 years old, was sentenced to be detained during His Majesty's pleasure.

A member of the public had lost his life in bringing criminals to justice, but his great sacrifice was not in vain. For when Jenkins and Geraghty were hanged, the police began to find an immense number of revolvers being dumped in shrubberies, in the

Thames, and in other places. The gunmen had been badly frightened.

21

Crime Reporters

ON THE THAMES EMBANKMENT, APPARENTLY HAV-ing no connection with Scotland Yard itself, is a barely noticeable green door. If you step through this door you will find yourself in a room with men playing cards perhaps, or reading, or just smoking and chatting. Along one wall of the room is a row of telephone booths, which may perhaps give you the clue to what these men are.

They are the crime reporters of the national newspapers. When there is a big murder story to be covered, you will of course find them on the scene of the crime. But between times they wait in the room inside the green door, kept in touch with events by the Yard's Press and Information Department, and in between, keeping in touch with their newspapers by telephone.

They, more than anyone else, are the link between the public and the police. In the old days it was the constable's duty to start a hue and cry after a criminal by calling on all passers-by to assist him. The police still raise the hue and cry, but now they call on the public through the newspapers and the

British Broadcasting Company, and very often that help gives the Yard quick and valuable results.

Sometimes the hue and cry through the newspapers results in a really sensational capture.

At about 8:30 on the ill-omened evening of Friday, February 13th, 1948, a young and promising aid to the C.I.D. named P.c. Nathaniel Edgar was making inquiries in a North London suburb.

Suddenly the silence of the quiet suburban road was shattered by shots. People came running. Someone dialed 999, and police cars quickly arrived. Edgar was found lying shot in the road, speechless. He was rushed to a hospital and died an hour later.

You will remember in Chapter Three the case of police constable Cole, and how the whole case hinged upon the single clue of a scratched chisel. The case of P.c. Edgar also hinged upon a single clue. Beside him as he lay dying was his notebook, in which he had apparently been writing when he was shot. It seemed to the Yard that he must have been questioning somebody, for there was an uncompleted note of a man's name and of a national registration card number.

That was all the Yard had to go on, and it was very little. The Yard traced the number, however, and found that it belonged to a man named Donald George Thomas. But where was Donald George Thomas? Who was he? Had he been with P.c. Edgar that night?

The clue of the chisel in the Cole case, you will

remember, was followed for a year before it led the police to the murderer. But in 1948 the police took a short cut. They set on the hue and cry through the newspapers.

They issued the name of Donald George Thomas to the newspapers. Of course they did not know who he was, and whether he had any connection with the murder. They said that they thought he might be able to assist them in their inquiries.

Thomas himself did not come forward, but a man named Winkless read the announcement in his paper, and reported to the police that Thomas had recently run away with Mrs. Winkless. He didn't know where they were, but he had no objection to a photograph of Mrs. Winkless being published.

The photograph was printed in the morning newspapers. At about 7:30 that morning, a boarding-house proprietress opened her paper and said excitedly to her husband, "Why, look! That's the woman who came in here last night with a man." She ran out into the street to look for a policeman, and within a few minutes the C.I.D. and uniformed police had the house covered.

Mrs. Winkless and her companion were still in their bedroom. They had not seen the morning paper yet, and knew nothing of Mr. Winkless's fateful call on the police. They had given orders for breakfast to be brought up to them at 8:30, and at 8:30 on the dot there was a knock on the door, and the comfortable rattle of a breakfast tray. Suspecting nothing, they opened the door.

There *was* a breakfast tray there—but on each side of the tray was a hefty policeman, and in front of the tray was a police inspector, a noted rugby player.

When Thomas saw the police, he dived for the bed, and the inspector dived for him, bringing him down with a full-blooded rugger "smother tackle" which enveloped his arms. That inspector was a brave man, for he was, of course, unarmed, whereas his opponent had under the bed pillow the loaded Lüger pistol with which Nat Edgar had been shot while he was questioning Thomas as a suspected housebreaker.

Nat Edgar had been killed on the evening of February 13th. Thomas was arrested on the morning of February 17th; just over three days, thanks to the newspapers, as against a year in the case of P.c. Cole 66 years before.

There is a strange little tailpiece to the story of Thomas, for though he was sentenced to death, he is still alive. The reason is that at the time of his trial a bill was before Parliament to suspend the death penalty for five years, and it had been announced that anyone sentenced to death while the bill was likely to be passed would have his sentence commuted to life imprisonment. Thomas was the first, and almost the last, murderer to escape, for shortly afterwards there was such an outcry against the suspension of the death sentence that the clause was dropped from the bill.

Another famous case in which the newspapers played their part was that of the "Mad Parson," John Edward Allen.

Allen was detained in Broadmoor, having been found guilty of child murder but insane. In July, 1947, he escaped from Broadmoor wearing, it was said, a parson's collar.

There were signs that he was making for London, which is a very convenient city to lose oneself in, and the police issued photographs of Allen to national newspapers, asking that people should keep a lookout for him.

Then the fun began. Police all over the country received hundreds of calls from people who said they had seen the Mad Parson, and many of these calls had to be followed up, to the acute embarrassment of many genuine parsons!

But Allen wasn't found. He had simply disappeared. Two years passed. A London evening newspaper thought it would be a good idea to republish Allen's photograph and remind people that he was still at liberty.

The proprietor of a bakery saw the photograph, and reported to the police that a man resembling the Mad Parson was working for him under the name of Kenneth Watts. C.I.D. officers had a good look at Kenneth Watts, identified him as the wanted man—and the Mad Parson's two-year spell of liberty was at an end.

There are many other instances of how the newspapers help the public to help the police. After the Second World War, there was an outbreak of armed hold-ups and robberies, due to the large number of pistols which had been brought home as souvenirs by servicemen and which were falling into the hands of criminals. The police appealed through the press and radio for these "souvenir" arms and ammunition to be handed in. As a result, for days police stations looked like international arsenals as good citizens brought along their treasured German and Italian and French and Japanese and American souvenirs.

Again, through newspapers, radio and traveling exhibitions, the police have been able to tell the public how to foil burglars and housebreakers. And of course there is the police force's biggest headache—not murder, not burglary, not anything which is considered a crime: but traffic accidents. More people are killed in traffic accidents in London in a month than murderers bump off in the Metropolis in a year. So the police, among other organizations, keep warning the public through the press to watch its step, to keep speed down, to look before crossing the road, to make sure that bicycle lamps are working. This is perhaps not spectacular work, like the hue and cry after a murderer. But it can save many more lives.

22

Routine Work

LET US END WHERE WE BEGAN, IN RADIO CAR 5D.

5D is coming up Bayswater Road now, late at night, the traffic lights glittering gold and green and red, the street lamps casting pools of light between the inky shadows from the park. The car loiters along, smoothly, effortlessly, the powerful engine barely a whisper. The two big men, the driver and the observer, with nearly 40 years' service between them, seem to sit back, idling like the engine. But they are not idling. Another car comes from a side turning into the main road. Nothing unusual about it, you would think. But just for a fraction of a second, as the driver changes gear, the car jerks forward, as if the driver were not quite used to the clutch.

"Hallo," says the observer of 5D. "Let's have a look at him."

5D turns on the other car's tail. The first car accelerates. 5D accelerates, too, draws alongside, and signals the driver to stop. He doesn't stop, he goes faster. 5D crowds him into the curb. Three men jump out as the car, still running, heads straight for a lamp post. The driver has jammed the throttle open, hoping the moving car will hit something, will make trouble for the police which will divert them from the chase. The car smashes into a lamp post and stops. The three men are running shadows along the dark street. They separate, dive down side turnings. The driver of 5D goes after one, the observer after another. The third man is lucky—for the moment.

The observer chases his man into a dark yard. There is no ray of light, and he has left his flashlight in the car. He can't see the man, doesn't know what awaits him in the darkness. The criminal may come quietly, or he may not. He may be some desperado like Donald George Thomas, the murderer of P.c. Edgar. The policeman goes on. The wanted man is standing at the very end of the yard, still, scarcely breathing. He doesn't fight—much. Only a wild kick, perhaps, to the stomach or the groin, which can do a policeman lifelong injury if he isn't trained to meet it. They go back together to the car. The driver of 5D is already there, with his man. 5D makes for Paddington Green Police Station.

There a call is put through to Information Room. A car with such and such a number—has it been reported stolen?

Information Room has heard nothing, but a note of the number goes out on the teleprinter to all police stations, informing them where the car is.

Then will Information Room find out from C.R.O. if anything is known about the two arrested men?

Yes, quite a lot is known. The driver has escaped

from Borstal and is wanted for six burglaries in Kent. The second man has a similar record.

When the two men see that the game is up, they are willing to talk about the third man. C.I.D. officers get on their way to interview *him*. . . .

In the morning an agitated citizen comes into a police station far away from Paddington Green. "My car was stolen in the night," he says. "I only missed it this morning. I came down from the north yesterday, to get married. The wedding's at eleven o'clock. We want the car to go away for our honeymoon. For heaven's sake, can't you do something about it?"

The station sergeant looks through the teleprinter messages from Information Room. Yes, Scotland Yard has already done something about it, the honeymoon is safe. The car is waiting at Paddington Green . . . just because the observer of radio car 5D had noticed that a driver wasn't quite used to the clutch.

Such little things give the criminal away. The keeper of a small hotel was found with his head battered in, his money stolen. At the moment of his death he had been sitting at his table, writing a bill for a customer we shall call James Robinson.

There is a 'phone call from the local C.I.D. to C.R.O. Anything known about James Robinson? Yes, he had been convicted of stealing from such small hotels, is wanted for several more offences. C.R.O. had his record, and there were his fingerprints. Near the murdered man was a milk bottle stained with blood—the implement with which the fatal blow had been struck. On the milk bottle were James Robinson's fingerprints. Such little things hang a man—James Robinson hadn't noticed, when he struck the blow, that his victim was writing out a bill for himself.

For twenty-four hours a day, 365 days in the year, the Metropolitan Police are on the alert to notice these little things. No policeman is ever off duty. A young policeman ill in bed heard the tinkle of glass. He leaped to the window, and was just in time to see a man's face, a wanted man, in the lamplight. Disregarding the fact that he was sick, that policeman was at the telpehone and reporting to Information Room in a matter of seconds.

Another constable and a sergeant of the C.I.D. were going home one day to lunch. As they boarded a trolley bus, they noticed a man whom they knew to be the brother of a deserter, a receiver of stolen property, climbing the stairs to the top deck. There might be nothing in it, of course; but they kept their eyes open. Presently they saw the man coming downstairs, his wanted brother with him. The detectives tried to jump off with the wanted man, but the deserter's brother barred their way, shouting "Run! Make for the river."

The sergeant forced his way past and gave chase. The two sprinted 150 yards, then the wanted man stumbled. He recovered himself, but the sergeant was almost on top of him. He turned, and landed heavy blows in the sergeant's face and stomach. The sergeant closed with him, and they rolled on the ground, struggling desperately. The sergeant got a painful kick in the groin, but he held on until the other detective arrived with the wanted man's brother.

They were near the river by that time, and the deserter asked if he might wash his bloody face. The sergeant agreed, while the constable kept a firm grip on him. Suddenly the brother assaulted the constable, making him lose his grip, and the deserter plunged into the river. The sergeant, badly hurt already, dived in after him, and there was another desperate struggle in the river.

The detective on the bank raced to the telephone, and asked Information Room to radio for a Thames Division launch. The sergeant was in desperate straits. Both the deserter and his brother were on top of him now, in deep water, trying to drown him. Fortunately the launch arrived in time, and threw ropes and lifebuoys to the struggling men. Suddenly the two brothers made for the opposite bank of the river and ran off. The sergeant somehow wearily dragged himself to the water's edge and collapsed, unconscious.

Both men were arrested later and given heavy sentences. The case was reported in the newspapers under the simple heading, "Arrest of a Deserter." Just that. Nothing more. The police do not care to boast about their heroism.

Perhaps when that sergeant recovered from his life-and-death struggle, he would be engaged in making inquiries about two little girls with pixie-hoods who were always running away from home, or about a lost bicycle perhaps, or a murder, a gambling den, or half-a-crown stolen from some-one's jacket in a cloakroom. Variety is the spice of the policeman's life, and nothing, however unusual, defeats him.

An old laborer once kept all his savings in a stocking, and the stocking was accidentally thrown on to the fire and burned. A life's savings gone in a flash. The Bank of England will replace notes if there is proof that the notes really have been burned. But the old man didn't even know how many he had had—perhaps £230, he thought. Scotland Yard found out for him. They searched among the debris for fragments of burned notes, for the little metal strips inserted in all Bank of England notes. They counted the strips, they conducted tests on the fragments, and they told the old man that he had had £280 in notes! What is more, they gave their expert evidence to the Bank, and the Bank agreed to replace the old man's lost wealth.

How much trouble the police would have been saved if the old man had been a bit more careful! How much less trouble for them if everyone kept a record of the numbers of their bicycles, their watches, their typewriters, anything else that is likely to be stolen, so that if they *were* stolen, the police could be given a clear-cut description, instead of vague guesses. Do *you* know the number of your bicycle? Do you always notify the police if you are going away for a few days, leaving the house empty, so that the policeman on his beat can pay special attention to it? Some people do. Many don't. The policeman's lot would be much happier, though perhaps less exciting, if everyone helped him by taking that little bit of extra trouble.

But the police always will help you, even though you don't always help yourself. A policeman is *always* on duty, looking after you.

Index